A Hebridean Naturalist

Peter Cunningham

Illustrations by
Andrew Miller Mundy

Published in Scotland in 1979 by Acair Limited, Cromwell Street Quay, Stornoway, Isle of Lewis.

ISBN 0-86152-025-4
© 1979 Text — Peter Cunningham
© 1979 Illustrations — Andrew Miller Mundy

Printed by Nevisprint Ltd., Fort William, Scotland.

For my family whose patience has been sorely tried.

"In nature's infinite book of secrecy, a little I can read."

Shakespeare — Antony and Cleopatra

Contents

Preface

Many people have derived a great deal of enjoyment over the years from Peter Cunningham's articles about Hebridean birds. His observation is sharp, his information surprisingly detailed, his style is lucid, and there is a nice sense of humour.

I feel that I have got more out of the articles than most because I have a blind spot where birds are concerned. It is possibly a defect of vision — I was never any good at games which involved dealing with a ball or a shuttle-cock in flight — and the birds are gone before I have really seen them. On the other hand it may be no more than a lack of patience and application. Either way I must do my bird watching by proxy, and that is why I get so much pleasure through Peter: he is such an admirable guide.

My one venture into bird watching was disastrous. One Sunday morning shortly before the war I saw a strange bird in my front garden on Matheson Road, Stornoway. I told a friend who commented, "I could understand some people seeing a bird like that on a Sunday morning, but you haven't even the excuse of a hangover." Fortunately he saw the birds himself, several of them, later in the day, in the Castle Grounds, and after some research, identified them as Bohemian Waxwings. I wrote a paragraph about them for the Gazette using the information borrowed from an encyclopedia that they are supposed to presage war, famine, or sudden death — which proved all too true a few months later. Imagine my surprise when I received a little monograph, published by someone in Edinburgh University, recording the visit of the waxwings that year to several parts of Scotland, and quoting me as authority for "an old Celtic myth" that they presage war, famine and sudden death.

Peter, unlike me, would have recognised the birds in the first place, and got his facts straight in the second. It is a privilege and a pleasure to write a preface to his book.

James Shaw Grant

Introduction

When all kinds of creatures, great and small, began to be brought to my office in the Custom House in Stornoway and all sorts of people began to bring their wild-life problems to me (sometimes they became my problems; a live golden eagle or cormorant, for example: even a dead grey seal or otter is not easily disposed of through Civil Service channels), it occurred to me that there were a great many of my fellow Islanders who wished sincerely to know more about the wild-life around them, in town and croft.

There was no natural history organisation in the Islands and I would feel frustrated from time to time at being unable to communicate, beyond a small circle of friends, my pleasure at seeing the first waxwing or an experience with a wounded peregrine falcon.

A regular column in the "Stornoway Gazette" seemed to be the answer. The editor was willing to comply with this solution and so "Nature Notes" were born. From the beginning I was aware that neither my knowledge nor that of most of my readers was of an academic standard. My mind had been disciplined, not by scientific training, but by King's Regulations and Admiralty Instructions and the labyrinthine directions of the Customs and Excise Department. I had, however, acquired a considerable library of natural history literature and had absorbed a small part of what concerned the Outer Hebrides. Where it is possible to acknowledge this borrowed information I have done so but a bibliography in such an unassuming book seems inappropriate.

Unlike all these writers I have lived continuously for nearly thirty years in Lewis and have travelled extensively during that time throughout the Long Island, including all the out-lying islands from North Rona and Sula Sgeir to Barra Head. I have been responsible for the "Scottish Birds" annual bird report in respect of the Outer Hebrides since its inception, except for two years, and, however undeservedly, have been credited with a wide (but superficial) knowledge of local wild-life.

Such is the power of the written word that scarcely a day passes without appreciation of my "Nature Notes" being received, verbally and literally. More than once it was suggested by friends, whose opinion I value, that these "Notes" should be given a more permanent form.

Hence this book.

I am grateful to the Editor and staff of the "Stornoway Gazette" for permission to reprint the "Notes" and for their cooperation and patience; to Andrew Miller Mundy for his splendid illustrations; to James Shaw Grant for his kindness in complying with my request for a preface; to Mrs MacKay for her elegant typescript and to all the friends I have made through my writing, whose encouragement has made it seem all worth while.

Peter Cunningham
Stornoway 26 December 1978

Enjoying Birds

This book is for those who enjoy watching birds. I stress the word 'watching', for although there must be a good deal of enjoyment to be obtained from a penetrating and self-denying study of a species, as shown by such books as Desmond Nethersole — Thompson's monographs, you and I can just watch and admire them, taking them as we find them, the most beautiful and highly developed creatures in the wild.

Specialists may argue with the last statement, but I believe that, while there are many mammals which may be described as beautiful and even perhaps a few insects such as butterflies and moths, all birds, with a few exceptions, may be so described and certainly they combine these attributes with a functional beauty that, when we bother to think about it, compels endless wonder.

Look closely, for example, at the next feather you find and see how exquisitely adapted it is for what it has to do. Examine the nest of a dipper or wren and remember that it was all done with a small beak.

Would that the trigger-happy shooter or the mischievous schoolboy took time to look properly at the wonder of creation he had in an instant destroyed — and repented.

Birds as we know them are far older than man, being more than 10 million years old, whereas I doubt if we would care to admit to our ancestors of one million years ago.

Ornithologists say there are 9,000 different species or kinds of birds in the world. Of these 468 are said to have occurred in the British Isles; and here, in the Western Isles, about 200 have been recorded and we provide a home for up to 100 of these.

We enjoy the company of many more different species than the city dweller of the mainland, for birds are all around us wherever we go. And they are cleaner too. See the sparkling irridescent plumage of the Hebridean starling or the snowy-white breast of our herring gull — two of our commonest and most easily watched birds — and try to forget the mess they make of your clothes line or new car.

One of the best places from which to watch birds is, of course, the motor car. Henry Ford must have been a bird watcher. Even the windows seem designed to support binocular or telescope at a convenient height by winding a handle. Some people may think that the motor car is merely a quick and comfortable means of getting from place to place, but we bird watchers know better.

The more advanced car-driving bird watcher can even watch birds under way, but passengers don't always appreciate the finer points of this art and tend to divert one's attention to oncoming traffic, which spoils one's enjoyment to a certain extent. I have derived much pleasure from watching birds from my car which would have eluded me had I been on foot.

Finally, birds may be enjoyed under so many different circumstances. They pass the time on a journey, or while listening to a bore. They relax one's mind when watched from the office window while wrestling with a problem and release the spirit of the convalescent from the confines of the sickroom.

Spring

"O, Man, if winter comes can spring be far behind?"

It is a perennial source of wonder to me that Nature, seemingly crushed under the iron heel of winter, betrays signs of inevitable spring wherever I look. It is a commonplace that the buds of the following year are to be seen as soon as the leaves of autumn fall but now these buds are beginning to swell and force themselves on our notice. People who have gardens will find crocus and daffodil leaves pushing up into a hostile environment. Visitors to the Stornoway Woods, known locally as the Castle Grounds, can pick branches of salmonberry whose pregnant buds will, in the warmth of a room, bear delicate pink flowers.

The ubiquitous cock blackbird dons his glossy black plumage the better to show off his splendid orange-yellow beak to prospective brown mates and to intimidate intruders.

The black-headed gull, having lived a lie all winter, begins to acquire flecks of dark brown which in another month or two will turn its white head black again (or to be strictly accurate, a very dark brown). Other gulls pair off and indulge in aggressive displays wherein the arched neck and down pointed bill are suddenly thrust upwards with much raucous noise.

Always gregarious creatures, the shags gather into large premarital flocks during January and February which, along with similar parties of red-breasted mergansers, can be seen in Stornoway harbour and other estuaries almost every day: so does Nature ensure that the survival of the species is not endangered by dispersion at mating time. Overhead, the courtship display of the raven takes one's breath away with its effortless virtuosity as the large two foot long bird does flip turns, rolling over on its back almost too quickly for the eye to follow.

Although they must have been there since the late summer it is only in spring that they came to our notice after the bareness of winter, those greyish, oddly shaped little objects clinging to the lintel of a door by a girdle of silk, above a window or in a garage or outhouse.

Another assurance of spring, but not this time altogether welcome, they contain an evolving white butterfly, the scourge of the cabbage patch.

The bright green caterpillar might have been seen climbing up a wall in the late summer until it found a suitable sheltered spot where it could spin a cocoon around itself in which the wonderful metamorphosis into a chrysalis and then a butterfly takes place.

Bird Song

"An eaglais shaor 's i's fheàrr,
An eaglais shaor 's i's fheàrr,
Na 'Moderates', na 'Moderates',
Cha'n fhiach iad, cha'n fhiach iad".

There are onomatopoeic rhymes and jingles galore in the Gaelic language which try to imitate the songs or sounds of birds.

The above praise of the Free Church at the expense of the "Moderates" is attributed to the song thrush, for example. Within the past few days (January 27th) the thrush has been slowly developing this theme and soon, if the weather is mild enough, the full song will be heard from roof-top or tree. Once March comes he will be accompanied by the blackbird's more melodious, flute-like: "Bun a ghuib, air a ghuib, bàrr a ghuib air a ghuib; eun-dubh air an nead, sheinn an lòn-dubh, eun-dubh, hó, hó, gràdh air na feadagan".

Unfortunately the many stray cats abroad will not leave her long on the nest or her mate singing.

Another song eagerly listened for afresh each spring is the descending strain with final flourish of the chaffinch, which has been rendered as "Kirvik, Kirvik, crodh an duine a's a' chorc". Soon after, from the Butt to Barra, wherever there are trees or bushes, the sweet, slender notes of the willow warbler may be heard as soon as he arrives from tropical Africa. I can find no translation for this song, but am not surprised since it would be difficult to express such a delicate pattern of sound even in mellifluous Gaelic.

In any case, this species must be a relatively recent visitor to the Western Isles for the nineteenth century authority, Harvie-Brown, makes no mention of it. Obviously the spread of treeplanting has encouraged it to venture forth from its initial stronghold in the Stornoway Woods.

"Groc, groc", says the raven, " 's e mo mhac sa' chrimeas na h-uain". "My son will pick the lambs". And he goes on saying it and begetting more sons thanks to the mistaken protection he enjoys in these islands.

Two familiar birds which sing all the year round are the robin and the wren. The former can even be heard at night when his bitter-sweet warble catches the listener unawares, while the tiny wren will astonish anyone approaching this cliff-haunting species on a still day with the volume of sound issuing from his three-and-a-half inch body, which visibly vibrates with the effort. The passage of many years has not dimmed the memory of wren song heard over the calm sea while still far from the cliff of Eilean Garbh or North Rona.

But, sad to say, none of these creatures is singing for our benefit. He is struggling for survival and for possession of his territory and mate and has evolved song as an effective means of communicating his title to others of his species who might be considering expropriation. Nevertheless, it is our good fortune that he does it so pleasingly.

I am indebted to Forbes *"Gaelic Names of Animals"* for some of the rhymes quoted above.

Bird Spotting

Some time ago three boys found an ailing buzzard in the Stornoway Woods and sought help in the right quarter where it was soon cured and released. It might easily, however, have suffered the fate of another buzzard, whose head and feet only were found about the same time near the Deer Park.

The first bird's saviours were only doing in their own small and highly commendable way what the Royal

Lapwing

Society for the Protection of Birds is trying to do for the birds of Britain. On such a scale, work of this nature costs money; money to purchase and maintain Reserves, money to pay wardens for these Reserves and to finance protection generally.

Recently, a scheme to raise funds for this work was promoted by the RSPB whereby bird-watchers canvassed sponsors to pay so much for each species spotted in the course of three hours.

Unfortunately, owing to a temporary indisposition, I was prevented from taking part with three friends. I did, however accompany them in spirit and wrote this putative account while confined to bed, of the birds I should have expected to see during a three-hour expedition centred on Stornoway.

I reckoned on spotting about fifty-five species on 3rd April, compiled as follows, taking no account of lucky sightings of rare or unseasonable birds. On the way to the Castle Grounds I should see house sparrows, a hedge sparrow, starlings, a robin or two, blackbird, thrush and chaffinch in the gardens I passed. A short walk up Willowglen would produce tree sparrows, goldcrest, blue and great tits, woodpigeon, pied-wagtail and the unwelcome hooded crow. No doubt the usual wren would dive for cover halfway up the stream and a grey wagtail appear in the upper reaches about this time.

Passing the rookery in Bayhead, I would set off by car for Point via the harbour where I would notch up collared doves, herring, lesser and greater black-backed and black-headed gulls, purple sandpiper on Goat Island; the usual Iceland or glaucous gull near Rolf Olsen's and in the harbour the expected shag, black and common guillemot would be offshore, bringing my score so far to twenty-seven. Jackdaws would be nesting in the chimneys of Matheson Road as I passed and the resident stonechat perched on the fence along the Sandwick Road. When the Braighe is reached the pencil comes out in earnest. If the local trigger-happy sportsman (?) hasn't been around recently I should find live long-tailed duck and scaup on the loch, lapwing, redshank and oystercatcher on the grass. To seaward, red-breasted mergansers, a cormorant and a red-throated diver feed while dunlin and ringed plover work the tide-line industriously.

No time to watch as usual though, and I press on to Aird to look for the little grebe on the loch there, together with mallard and teal. Tufted duck, goldeneye, common gulls and the local raven reward a search toward Tiumpan Head where a quick glance over the Minch reveals fulmars, gannets and kittiwakes, while a rock dove flashes past along the cliffs.

The first wheatear of the year, all the way from Africa, is an exciting bonus.

Almost two hours have gone so I hurry back through Stornoway to take the Tolsta road, noting in passing rock pipits at the Braighe and meadow pipits at Tong, skylark and corn bunting and a flock of twite near Coll, to look for the usual whooper swans on the saltings and eider offshore.

Beating the clock by a few minutes I am back in town with fifty-eight species in the bag. Given more time and some luck another dozen could probably have been added. It should be said that I enjoyed perfect conditions for my journey and it would be interesting to see what my friends saw on a wet and windy day.

Time to Stand and Stare

The afternoon I am about to describe took place within a few miles of Stornoway, but it could have happened on almost any beach on the west coast of the Long Island in the spring of the year.

I had set out to record, if I was lucky, the first tern of the year. By this time, I was running out of 'firsts' for 1977, most of our summer visitors having already arrived, but I still had to meet my first Arctic and common terns, Arctic skua, flycatcher and corncrake.

On my way to the beach, I met a bird-watching friend who told me that he had seen his first tern a week before. Now, according to my records, this was very early and could have been a bird on passage.

Two large, dark birds were fishing close to inshore when I arrived and for a while I enjoyed wonderful views of two great northern divers in full summer plumage, their size, black heads and whitish collars distinguishing them from nearby red-throated divers. I was interested to note how much darker was the bill than that of the possible white-billed diver I once thought I saw in January, notwithstanding the latter being in winter dress.

Moments later, I heard the querulous cry of a 'comic' tern (That is, either an Arctic or a common tern, these being very difficult to separate in flight at a distance) and looked up to see one being chased by a piratical Arctic skua, thus achieving two 'firsts' with one glance. This skua is a parasite on the tern family and usually arrives in this country at the same time, joining the prevenient great skua or bonxie on the local breeding grounds, the latter preying on the larger gulls.

Another object of my outing was to look for the American green-winged teal which had frequented the

area since March but no teal were visible, having separated to breed no doubt.

There were many other birds, however, to make up for the loss. Three whimbrel, smaller cousins of the curlew, with shorter beak and striped crown, were feeding in a pool. Several dunlin in reddish-brown breeding plumage, their black bellies picking them out from other waders, trilled musically as they searched the wet sand for food.

The banks of rotting seaweed held a store of good things for rock pipits and my first white wagtails of the year. Most people know the pied or water wagtail whose dapper black and white attire is becoming a common sight in these islands and they might be forgiven for overlooking these migrant white wagtails which pass through each spring on their way to breed in Iceland or northern Europe.

One should examine any wagtail seen feeding on the shore in spring or autumn for it is likely to be one of the latter, whose grey back is the most conspicuous difference from our own pied wagtail in the breeding season. All the birds I have mentioned as migrants perform almost incredible feats of endurance in their journeys to and from their breeding grounds. The tern I had seen had just flown 10,000 miles from the Antarctic, the great northern diver and the others were about to fly off over hundreds of miles of ocean to the very lake or marsh where they were born.

How, I thought to myself as cars and motor-cycles hurtled past, can one suppress a sense of wonder at the workings of Nature and, with W.H. Davies, ask "What is this life if, full of care, we have no time to stand and stare".

Rooks

Though few inhabitants of these islands outside the Parish of Stornoway will have seen a rook, for they are creatures of limited range and fixed habits, they are a common sight in the fields surrounding the town and in the Castle Grounds at all times of the year. In spring their raucous call greets every visitor to the Grounds and every pedestrian in Church Street and Lewis Street. Promptly at dusk every evening in winter they stream across the sky above Stornoway to their roosts in the Woods, having fed all day on seeds and insects from Laxdale to Back. Their favourite food is said to be wireworms and leather-jackets, the grubs of daddy-long-legs, so crofters and farmers regard them as friends, and the grain they eat as well-earned reward. The rook can be distinguished from the other members of the crow family by his scaly, grey face and hoarse, unmusical cawing. He is not a carrion eater nor does he prey on lambs like his cousins, the ill-smelling hooded crow, the carrion crow and the raven.

It is written that Sir James Matheson tried unsuccessfully to introduce rooks into his newly planted woods in the mid-nineteenth century but several thousand birds arrived on the west coast of Lewis in October 1893, of which some 4,000 found their way to the woods where the survivors began to breed a year or two later. By 1902 there were over a hundred nests which increased by 1945 to 170. In 1954, when I started to count the nests annually, there were 17 near the Gardener's Cottage and 200 in the conifers on the slopes of Gallows Hill. A gale in 1955 destroyed this rookery, the enormous windage caused by huge agglomerations of nests, tier upon tier, proving too much for the shallow roots. In 1956 two pairs were brave enough to build in the Percival Square trees but the urban hurly-burly must have been too much for them for they gave up in 1968.

By 1960 the displaced rooks had joined the Gardener's Cottage rookery and have since spread northwards along the Bayhead Burn, almost to the Golf Club House. The disruption of 1955 resulted in the establishment of a rookery in the Free Church trees which numbered 36 nests by 1962. The offending branches with nests were, however, cut off, and the rooks have not since returned.

By and large, the total number of nests in the Castle Grounds and in the town has remained fairly constant at almost 200 though it is difficult to make an accurate count of occupied nests where they have begun once again to form large accumulations of nesting material.

Early Birds

The raven is one of our earliest nesters and I visited a pair as usual in mid-March to see how they were getting on. The hen was sitting in the huge nest under an overhanging cliff in a typically inaccessible position. The untidy mass of heather was, however, so conspicious that it was not difficult to spot the nest which, in any case, was well advertised by great white splashes of excreta.

The cock bird soon appeared and was joined by the hen in an absorbing display of frustrated emotion. Both birds flew restlessly about the cliff face and came in turn to within ten yards of me, when they would turn up and toss aside clumps of grass and lichen. Now and again one or other would chase a fulmar or herring gull for no apparent reason for it was nowhere near the nest.

Such behaviour, known to biologists as "displacement activity" often occurs when a creature is subjected to external pressure and can be observed in the commonest birds as when, for example, they commence violent preening in an interval of altercation with a rival.

A few days later the first of our summer visitors began to arrive from their distant winter quarters in warmer climes. I look every year for the wheatear about the end of March and was not therefore surprised to hear from friends that the first wave of migrant wheatears had been seen on 24th March and on succeeding days. But it is our own breeding birds that really count, and so when a dapper grey head with a jet black eyestripe appeared above a rock by the loch at Garry on 27th March, I metaphorically shook hands as with an old friend, for a pair always nest not far from the shore amongst the rock and heather of the steeply rising hillside.

He, for it is the cock who usually in my experience arrives first, must have found the flurries of snow that day a chilling welcome after the hot sands of the Sahara.

In North Tolsta another Mediterranean visitor was resting with his herring gull cousins in a field. This was a lesser blackbacked gull, whose dark grey wings and bright yellow legs distinguished him. He spends our winter in the Mediterranean and off West Africa. The first lesser blackback of the year always recalls wartime passages to and from Freetown when the offshore winds, indescribably redolent of tropical Africa, stirred my youthful imagination.

Rallus Aquaticus

It all began one day not long ago when an acquaintance appeared on my doorstep with a box. He opened the box and showed me a headless kiwi on a cabbage leaf. You know the bird on the shoe polish tin. At least that's what it looked like until I poked it (not a practice to be recommended, by the way, as I have discovered with, for example, a cormorant). A head ending in a long beak appeared from nowhere and eyed me balefully. I was looking at my first live water rail.

The whole thing was ridiculous from the start for the bird had walked in his back door and water rails are just about as common in the Outer Hebrides as the "British" kind!

I promised to look after the bird and release it in due course, for it appeared to be quite uninjured and while all this was going on the bird had decided to go to sleep again. All the rail family prefer to walk rather than fly and the Minch had obviously been too much for this member.

I prepared to photograph it from a discreet distance, taking elaborate precautions lest it escape. I needn't have bothered; it went to sleep again, this time on one leg and now resembled nothing so much as a small upright feather duster. I approached closer with each shot and had to poke it each time to show that it was really a bird with head. It was quite plain that it took a dim view of the whole business for it lost no time in going to sleep again. Indeed, I was hard put to it to get a snap before head disappeared under wing, even when I was about fourteen inches away with full flash.

Thereafter, the bird remained sound asleep on my table for the rest of the afternoon, a source of wonder and amusement to all who saw it, and did not really wake up until the following day when it was successfully released near a suitable dense growth of grass and reed, into which it quickly became lost to sight.

Everyone is familiar with the voice of the land-rail or corncrake which keeps some of us awake in May or June, but few have seen a live one as rails are among the shyest birds we have — or so they say — but try scraping a stiff card across the teeth of a comb within earshot of a calling corncrake in early May and you will bring it to your feet. But make sure no one is watching you. It is difficult to give a convincing explanation to the uninitiated.

Round the Western Isles in Four Hours

When I was offered a 'pier-head jump' as navigator on an aerial survey of the wildfowl of the Western Isles one week, it didn't take me long to make up my mind to accept the unique opportunity of a bird's eye view of my 'parish'.

I pushed thoughts of Tommy Darkie's forced landing on Eigg to the back of my mind and boarded the little single-engined aircraft along with the pilot and two scientists from Aberdeen University at 1.30 p.m.

Although my main function was to ensure that we flew over all the possible sites where such species as eider and long-tailed duck might be found, no easy task when one is moving at 100 mph, 500 feet up and unable to stop and look at signposts. I soon found myself intrigued by the problems of identifying birds from above instead of below and of counting them in the few seconds they were within my field of view. Size was also difficult to judge until one had established the relative magnitude of, say, razorbill and gannet.

Before we left Stornoway, the improvement in the local weather, which had brought my companions from Aberdeen, was also releasing large flocks of geese from days of thraldom by adverse winds. We must have counted upwards of a thousand geese in three great skeins, pointing their enormous lop-sided arrowheads to the north-west and Iceland, and we were to encounter many more such flocks during our flight.

Unfortunately, most of the long-tailed duck had also left our shores but there was still much to engage our attention. Less than a quarter of an hour after taking off we were flying below the clifftops of the Shiant Isles to which I had often struggled by sea for three hours. Southwards we flew by East Loch Tarbert and Lochmaddy where we shared their element in passing with a pair of magnificent golden eagles, and thence by the lonely cliffs and hillsides of South Uist.

All the time we were in continuous communication by radio with the Air Traffic Controllers at Stornoway and Benbecula and I was both impressed and comforted by their painstaking concern in our progress.

Many eider were scattered over the sound of Barra and in Castlebay itself, the drakes conspicuous in their piebald plumage, but little else. However, the unfamiliar landscape unfolding as we passed Vatersay and Mingulay and the islands towards Barra Head held me enthralled.

We turned now and headed north up the west coast in order to refuel at Benbecula before the aerodrome closed. Permission to fly through the forbidden zone adjacent to the rocket-range having been obtained, a busy spell ensued with calls from both sides of 'eider ten', 'shelduck two', 'long-tailed duck five', etc.

The continuous banking turns proved too much for the young scientist alongside me and he became airsick. I was glad I was wearing my hat and that it was his own which proved to be the nearest receptacle!

Shelducks

From Benbecula we were soon over more new territory for me, the Monach Isles, whose apparently fertile acres were marred by the sad remains of former dwellings and a forlorn lighthouse, now blind and dumb.

But I think I worked my passage for the rest of the flight over Valley Sound and the Sounds of Taransay and Scarp and Loch Roag, where the intricate pattern of islands and inlets, with the continual turning and bad visibility proved my local knowledge to be a useful saver of time and temper.

Crossing Lewis a couple of hundred feet up above the Achmore road we exchanged waves with passing motorists who were doubtless envious of our independence of Lewis roads, and gave at least one elderly raven something to think about as we flew past him.

A' Chorra-Ghritheach

I have been asked from time to time the origin of the resonant, unearthly screech which is sometimes heard on a still evening from the foreshore of the harbour at Stornoway or of an estuary. This is the alarm call of the grey heron (corra-ghritheach) a stately, crane-like bird which can often be seen by loch, stream or sea-shore in these Islands.

About three feet tall and upright in posture, it stands motionless on long legs waiting for some unsuspecting creature to come within range of its yellow dagger of a beak. The raucous call may also be heard at any time when it is disturbed, for it is a nervous bird and difficult to approach, although I have often got close to one in a car and, in the old days, when travelling by train to Kyle by Loch Carron.

Heron

Once on the wing, it will withdraw its neck into its shoulders and stretch its legs beyond its tail, thus presenting quite a unique profile.

There was no breeding record for the Western Isles until 1902 when, according to "Birds of Scotland" (Baxter and Rintoul), a pair bred near the Lewis and Harris border on a rock called Tarsnig.

I have been unable to identify this place on the Ordnance Survey map: perhaps someone who lives in the area will enlighten us. Now, small colonies and single nests may be found the length and breadth of these Islands, mostly on sea cliffs as at Carloway, Little Loch Roag, Loch Erisort, Cliasay Mór in Lochmaddy and Lochboisdale.

Small heronries almost at ground level on stunted trees are to be found on islets on fresh water lochs; for example at Loch Keose in Lewis and Loch Hornary in Grimsay. There was said to be a heronry of 30 nests on Barra in 1945 and it would be interesting to learn if it still exists.

A predominantly tree-nesting species on the mainland, few herons use such a site here. They nest in the Castle Grounds and a few pairs have nested in a belt of conifers at Horgabost in Harris.

Four or five sky-blue eggs are laid in March and a beautiful picture they make against the seaweed-strewn ledge and the dark cliff.

The Jews regarded the heron as an unclean bird ("corra-ghlas" in Deuteronomy 14:18) and when one considers its normal diet of eels, frogs and mice one can see their point, but it was probably a favourite ingredient in the bubbling cauldron of Macbeth's witches. It was a common quarry of the medieval falconer. Here, however a lack of amphibians make them more dependent on fish but the number of eels they must account for compensates for the small fish they take.

Herons are called cranes in some parts of the country but the true crane is almost a foot taller, flies with outstretched neck and is very rare here, one only having been recorded — near Stornoway in 1904.

Herons, their young and eggs are fully protected throughout the year and it is an offence to kill them or take the eggs.

Flamingoes in Western Isles

"Very true", said the Duchess: "flamingoes and mustard both bite. And the moral of that is — "Birds of a feather flock together". 'Only mustard isn't a bird', Alice remarked"

And flamingoes don't seem to flock together in this part of the world, for three solitary individuals have turned up in the Western Isles in the past 70 years.

The first recorded instance was in 1918 when a flamingo spent the summer in Broadbay in Lewis. The next enjoyed, we hope, a similar sojourn at Northton in Harris in 1969. I wasn't around when the first came on the scene and the second wasn't around when I came on the scene. So I was sceptical when an acquaintance from Bragar in Lewis informed me one evening in April 1977 that there was a flamingo at the bottom of her croft!

My delight and surprise can be imagined when, even from a mile away I descried the pink form of an undoubted flamingo. Keeping carefully out of sight we approached the bird until we had run out of cover and found ourselves less than a hundred yards from the huge wader. She was so stunningly beautiful that I cannot help referring to the bird from now on as female.

Previous experience of captive birds led me to expect a mainly white bird but her plumage shaded from the palest rose to bright carmine. The delicate plumes cascading over her folded wings were delicate pink. A thin line of black along her flank marked her primary wing feathers.

During most of our stay she was perched on an incredibly long, thin, grey leg, the 'knee' joint of which was sealing-wax red, her supple swan-like neck folded between her wings as she rested.

But the most extraordinary feature of an altogether extraordinary bird was her beak. From time to time she would begin to feed in the shallows, stirring up the sand

and mud with a treading action of her pink, webbed feet, as though 'marking time' in a military sense, and sweeping her peculiar beak upside down and from side to side sifting out the algae and other minute food from the turbid water.

Four species of flamingo breed in the Old and New World. From the absence of any ring on her legs and her rosy-red plumage we may infer that our bird is a greater flamingo from the West Indies.

When we had retired discreetly from the scene, a van was driven over the machair to within 50 yards of the bird. The occupants jumped out for a better view and the flamingo immediately and not surprisingly took off and flew out to sea. By their selfish and thoughtless action they had probably deprived many other people of an interesting spectacle.

But her hasty departure proved that she was not an 'escape' although we weren't able to confirm the Duchess's contention that she bit.

A Cuckoo in the Nest

So many folk have asked me about cuckoos that I feel it is time I wrote something about this unique bird. Not so long ago the male cuckoo was regarded as slightly immoral, forming an irregular union with various small birds of opposite gender and giving rise to such literary allusions as 'cuckold'. What part the female cuckoo was supposed to play no one could say. Not until a photograph was obtained of the female cuckoo placing a naturally acquired egg in a nest was the cuckoo enigma solved and salacious rumours laid to rest.

It is now accepted that pairing takes place soon after the male and female cuckoo arrive in this country from their winter quarters in Africa. We in the Western Isles first hear the male's familiar call towards the end of April or in early May while he is seeking a mate or defending his territory.

Since it is a woodland species, we usually encounter it in the neighbourhood of such trees as we have left, though the call is often heard from a rock. Its hawk-like profile leads to confusion with the merlin here, but the long spotted tail, more buoyant flight and the young cuckoo's white spot on nape distinguish the cuckoo. Normally grey, the female and young can occasionally be brown.

When the female has chosen the "wet nurse" for her single egg, generally in these islands a meadow pipit, referred to as "gocoman", she lays an egg similar in size and shape and colour to that of the "wet nurse's". No one, so far as I know, can say how she manages to imitate eggs of different species, though it has been suggested that some cuckoos may specialise.

I was shown a nest at Dalbeg, filled to overflowing with one half-grown cuckoo, whose huge orange-yellow gape greeted our prying fingers. The four original occupants of the nest, unfledged wheatears, lay dead outside. It is said that this monstrous, gluttonous changeling has a tender spot on his back. Usually hatching out first and growing much faster he finds his way to the bottom of the nest and when an egg or nestling lands on the spot, the cuckoo with a convulsive heave, ejects it from the nest. The deprived parents adopt the cuckoo and feed it until it grows many times larger than themselves. I hope to return to this area to discover whether this female cuckoo again chooses wheatears as foster parents.

The adult cuckoos, relieved of the burden of parenthood, cease calling in late summer and return soon after to their winter quarters. The final cuckoo mystery is how the young birds, which do not migrate until after their parents, whom they have never seen, find their own way to join them in Africa.

Eilean an Fhraoich or Eilean an Rainich?

The last day on which heather burning may be carried out is 15th April unless, by written consent, the landlord extends the season until April 30th. This is a sensible and humanitarian rule which every landlord and Grazings Committee should take to heart.

Too often in the past, irresponsible and heartless individuals have set fire to tinder-dry moorland in May or June and found the fire gaining the upper hand or callously abandoned the conflagration. Acres of vegetation are consequently destroyed. The peat itself is often ignited so that the next gale fans the glowing peat and starts a fresh fire.

Regeneration is impossible, seed having been devoured in the holocaust, and nothing but bracken which is poisonous to cattle and not very good for sheep, can grow in the desert left by the fire, followed by erosion as the top-soil is washed away by ensuing rains. In short, such fires are pure vandalism and in the long term their effect on these islands may be disastrous.

It was probably fire which destroyed what was left of the scrub woodland covering the Hebrides after the present blanket of peat was formed. Only islands in the bigger lochs retain to the present day a cover of birch, alder and rowan.

Muirburn, properly carried out, can undoubtedly benefit a moor, provided no part of it is burnt more often than every twenty years and provided each fire is carefully controlled and contained.

There are three main types of heather found in these islands. Bell heather (Erica cinerea) and cross-leaved heath (Erica tetralix) flower in June and July on drier ground and are followed in August by the much more common ling (Calluna vulgaris), the glory of the moor in all its countless shades of red and purple.

Many birds find shelter and nest in this heather and fires after April 15th can cause untold suffering and distress to grouse, duck, snipe, plover and all the other species which frequent our moors.

I have encountered many instances of this, the worst being on 22nd April 1967, when I visited Eilean na h-Iolaire on Laxavat Iosal near Carloway. This attractive tree-girt islet was covered with tall rank heather, useless for grazing, but a haven for greylag geese, generations of which had bred in safety in its depths, laying their eggs in early April. On that day however, it was a hideous, blackened eyesore of charred stems and bare peat. The geese had disappeared, never to return. Only in high summer is the desolation hidden under a mass of indestructible bracken and no birds nest.

May I appeal to all who value our wonderful tracts of beautiful and nutritious heather, our wild-life and, not least, delicious heather-nourished native mutton, to do all in their power to prevent haphazard and out of season burning and accidental fires during peat-cutting.

Snipe

Summer

A Nest of Singing Birds

Several years ago, a home-made nest box was set up on a north-facing wall so that it would be shaded from the mid-day sun, but apart from an occasional inquisitive starling, no bird even looked over this desirable residence. Each year a pair of blackbirds, for whom it was intended and eminently suitable, built in clematis or cypress and lost their young to cats.

About the middle of April, however, the hen blackbird was seen to be carrying grass into the box and by the 20th the nest was complete. Five days later she was sitting on four mottled blue eggs. The box had been placed so that it could be watched from a window at a distance of only 20 feet without disturbing the bird; in fact she became quite used to our passing below and would follow our progress with apparent interest. If she left the nest during the next week, no one saw her, nor was her glossy black mate seen to come near her. He was too busy keeping other cocks at bay with his glorious song from the rooftop. But by 1st May, the brown hen had begun to make brief sorties for a few minutes and it was amusing to see the cock suddenly appear at the nest now and look around as if to say, "Now where's she gone?"

On 6th May, both birds began to bring beakfuls of worms to the box. The eggs had hatched; three of them anyway, and we never discovered what happened to the fourth. The hen was meticulously tidy even to the extent of swallowing the tiny white droppings of the chicks so she probably ate the eggshells too. Otherwise the conspicuous droppings and shells would have betrayed the presence of the young to predators.

At the end of a week of assiduous feeding, three gaping beaks appeared over the edge of the nest every time the parents whistled their arrival. The latters' absences grew longer and one day the hen was away much longer than usual, the cock calling in an agitated manner which indicated the presence of another infernal stray cat. We all feared the worst had happened until, to everyone's relief, she appeared again.

Soon the young could be seen to be partly feathered and then in no time at all, exercising vigorously, if dangerously, on the edge of the nest. Then the first one threw himself into an adjacent tree on 18th May, followed the next day by his siblings.

Now the parents' troubles really started. The three young birds dispersed through the garden, keeping up a continuous querulous "I'm hungry" call. While gardening, I often had the cock, normally wary, come within inches of me to pick up worms in the manner of a robin. The still tail-less young were unable to steer a premeditated course and there was an alarming thump on the window one evening when one, deceived by the reflection of the setting sun, flew into the glass. Happily, he was only stunned and seemed to have recovered after being lifted to the safety of the bird table.

The hen must have found the nestbox satisfactory for she rebuilt the nest on 24th May and by the 27th, was sitting on four eggs again. No sooner had the eggs hatched however, than she abandoned them and I am sorry to report that she has not yet returned.

A Woodland Walk

A party of six girls and boys from Leverburgh School, Harris, visited the Stornoway Woods on a Saturday in May. Brought by a sympathetic member of the community from an area where trees are rather thin on the ground, the children's principal object was to see woodland birds in their natural habitat.

I had rashly undertaken to show them birds unique to the Stornoway Woods and we set off through that part which derives its name from the same source as the village whence they came, Lady Lever Park. In vain we searched for blue and great tits and goldcrests; almost every bird we encountered seemed to be a robin or a chaffinch.

In passing, we discussed the rarest and commonest tree, flower and bird, pausing to examine the only plant of green hellebore and to listen to, probably the only chiffchaff. The many sycamores, carpets of lesser celandine and hosts of robins, we took in our stride, although it was difficult to decide whether the rook was the commonest bird.

Kestrel

From Lady Lever Park we passed over the golf course where they witnessed for the first time some splendid but abortive efforts to place a small white ball in a cavity in the ground with implements, ill-adapted, one might think, for the purpose.

Praiseworthy measures by the Stornoway Estate Trustees to overcome years of comparative neglect by felling dead trees, erecting sheep-proof fences and clearing paths long overgrown by rhododendrons, were noted and admired.

A profusion of young seedling trees and wild flowers, hitherto devoured by omnivorous, invading sheep, carpeted the woodland floor. The clearance of these pests by proper fencing and the opening up of the canopy by thinning will allow such plants to become established and enrich the woods for all to enjoy.

The value of the woods as a source of enjoyment and knowledge needed no emphasis to these children, whose only trees are a few gaunt, stunted sycamores in Glen Rodel, remnants of a fine wood planted, probably last century.

I demonstrated how the specially mild climate existing in the shelter of these century old Stornoway trees allowed tender plants like azalea and Gunnera manicata, the 'wild rhubarb', to flourish and increase and how a wealth of unusual and even rare trees and shrubs, surviving unaided by the expert attention they would require elsewhere, could rival more professionally maintained collections on the mainland.

Nests

When I see great fires burning on the moors of the Uists and Lewis and think of all the wild creatures perishing in their paths, my mind turns to Balaam's oracle to the Kenites: "Your refuge, though it seems secure, your nest, though set on the mountain crag, is doomed to burning . . . " Like Cain, too many of us are bent on destruction without counting the cost but we shall all reap the whirlwind. The hideous blackened waste left by a moor fire after dry weather will doubtless be sterile and eventually colonised by useless bracken or washed away by winter rains.

In order to divert my thoughts from the nests of meadow pipit and golden plover and the rest devoured by the fires, I begin to reflect on the variety of nests I have come across in my time.

Although no British bird can rival the weaverbird in its skill, and it is difficult to believe that the house sparrow with its untidy, often pirated, nest is one of this talented family, we can find many examples of almost incredibly intricate nest-building among our own birds.

Robins are of course, well known for their curious taste in sites for their nests. The most original in my recollection was one I was shown by an employee of James MacKenzie's old shop in Cromwell Street. In a small yard at the back hung an old rope in coils, once used to hoist goods to an upper floor, and in the coils a robin had built its nest.

While the present taxi-ways at Stornoway aerodrome were under construction, a ringed plover had laid its eggs on a piece of land from which the turf had been removed prior to excavation by an immense earth-

Ringed plover

moving machine. So accustomed had the little bird become to the noise of this earth-shaking monster that she sat tight while work was proceeding but left her nest when it stopped, not to return until the noise recommenced. The considerate workmen had placed a sheet of corrugated iron to mark the nest and protect it from accidental destruction and excavation of the nest site was delayed until the young had hatched out.

Devotion of another sort was shown by a little grebe which built its twelve inch wide nest of floating weed in the reeds of Loch Tuamister near Shawbost in 1959. The mass was unrecognisable as a nest until I removed a covering of weeds to reveal five eggs. On my approach the bird had carefully concealed them before ensuring her own safety.

A Journey through the Hebrides

At the end of May 1977 I had the opportunity, in the course of my duties, to travel by land and sea to the Uists and Barra and managed to fit the journey in before the end of our summer. The flat calm enabled me, during the passage from Tarbert to Lochmaddy via Uig, to forget that I had a stomach and to concentrate on looking for birds. Apart from our escort of several herring and two lesser black-backed gulls, the commonest bird seen was probably the puffin. These little auks with multi-coloured, parrot-like beaks were everywhere, diving in a panic as the ship's wash overwhelmed them.

It was Puffinus puffinus we were looking for and I do not mean two puffins but the Manx shearwater, which rejoices in this tautonymous name. Although it can be confused with the fulmar petrel in bad light, for both species have the same graceful, skimming flight, with scarcely a wing-beat, the former is normally easily recognised, being black above and white below. Half-way across the Minch we did come upon a small flock, whose summer home was probably not far away on the island of Rhum.

Rising early next morning we motored north to the Balranald Nature Reserve at Hougharry in North Uist, surprising a short-eared owl just outside Lochmaddy.

The red-necked phalarope winters in the South Atlantic and breeds mainly in the Arctic. One of its southerly nesting grounds is in the Uists where it is a gradually diminishing species and one of our rarest birds. We were therefore delighted to see the first arrival and to watch this delicate little wader with its slender neck and needle-like beak as it pirouetted in the shallows of a loch to stir up food. Perhaps the two or three pairs surviving will succeed this year in bringing forth young, despite the oppressive attention of the more importunate bird-watchers and predators.

Some spare time was usefully spent on the outskirts of the other Reserve at Loch Druidebeg in South Uist where more recent arrivals from the sunny south were encountered in the shape of spotted flycatchers which do not seem to have been recorded in South Uist before.

Among the trees and bushes surrounding Grogarry Lodge two or three more were busily feeding in the manner peculiar to the flycatcher family, though the lightish throat and upright posture are good guides, quick, darting flights from a branch to catch a flying insect and returning at once to the same branch.

We couldn't pass Peninerine without having another look at the famous and locally unique Steller's eider and we were lucky to find it in its usual place a few yards offshore where it seemed to be courting a common eider duck. The bright sunlight and calm sea allowed a splendid opportunity to study its colourful plumage, which differed in some ways from the book.

Similar weather during the crossing to Barra and our brief stay there revealed the island's considerable charms at this time of year. The golden gorse blazed in the bright sun in unexpected corners of the east coast but we were just too late to see the marvellous primrose carpet at Eoligarry.

Wren

Two swallows were active on the shore near the pier and we wondered if they were carrying mud to a nest in an empty house towards which they flew. It was so warm that I took my work outside onto the machair but found concentration too difficult in the company of nearby corncrakes, cuckoos and corn buntings.

Eoligarry House, once the home of a noted ornithologist, MacGillivray, whose collection of mounted birds may be seen in Aberdeen University's splendid museum, is now no more, I was sad to note. But perhaps the gradual and pathetic dilapidation of what must have been an imposing mansion was better brought to an end.

Skuas

I much prefer the American name, jaeger, for this family of rakish predators. Jaegar comes from the German word for a hunter, which describes perfectly this sky highwayman, who gains his livelihood by hunting down other birds and stealing their food and which is therefore only remotely connected with elegant knitwear. Our name, skua, comes on the other hand from the Old Norse name for the species, skufr. There are four species of skua, all of which spend our winter at sea in the north and south Atlantic.

Two of these, the great and Arctic skua, breed in these islands but the long-tailed and pomarine skuas visit us only on passage. The great skua, or bonxie as it is known in Shetland and Fair Isle where it is very common, is the largest, nearly as big as a great black-backed gull, and dark brown all over except for a prominent white flash on each wing. Their southernmost colonies are in Lewis where they nest on flat wet moorland in exiguously lined hollows in the drier parts. They are very shy and leave the nest on the distant approach of a stranger, when their nest, with its two or three brown eggs can be found only by assiduous searching in the face of low-flying attacks by the parents in succession, pressed home with alarming precision.

The smaller, more graceful Arctic skua is commoner and more widespread and had been found breeding in North Uist. Their plaintive, miaowing calls remind me of a cat. This skua has the Latin specific name, parasiticus, which relates to its habit of chasing terns with acrobatic skill until the latter disgorge their last meal of sand-eels or small fish, and dexterously intercepting the disgusting mess before it reaches the water. Anyone, with time to spare in summer, can observe this operation at, say, the Braighe or Port of Ness.

This skua was formerly called Richardson's skua after the Scottish naturalist, Sir John Richardson (1787 - 1865) of Dumfries who served on Arctic explorations with Perry and Franklin.

The long-tailed skua is, for most of us, a picture in a book, but a correspondent has recently informed me that he watched a flock of twenty-four passing northwards offshore at Balranald in North Uist.

This skua was formerly called Buffon's Skua after the French naturalist, Georges Louis Leclerc (1707 - 1788) later created Comte de Buffon by Louis XV. Its long slender, central tail feathers, extending five to eight inches beyond the others, give it its name and distinguish it from the Arctic skua. The last member of the family is the pomarine skua, or as it used in more leisurely times to be known, the pomatorhine skua, on account of the bone formation covering the nostrils. This species was said by J.A. Harvie-Brown to frequent "the harbour of Carloway . . . and the seas over the great codbanks between that and the Flannan Islands." It is distinguished by broad, twisted central tail feathers.

A Greenshank

Two of the most excitable birds are the redshank and the greenshank, smallish waders with, as their names suggest, red and green legs respectively. The former, like the poor, are always with us and spoil many a day's bird-watching with their nervous clamour when disturbed, alarming all other birds in the vicinity.

The greenshank is mainly a summer visitor and, except on the feeding grounds in estuary or foreshore, it is one of our most elusive breeding birds. As far as I am aware, only one nest of this species has been found in Lewis, where it is found most commonly. Once on 13th June 1957, I came across two young greenshanks which was almost as rewarding as finding a nest since the young birds leave the nest a very short time after hatching.

On this occasion, I had received information from the RSPB in London that an egg-collector was planning to visit Lewis to look for greenshanks' eggs and others. Somehow his plans had been obtained by the RSPB and these included a reference to breeding greenshanks in a part of Lochs. My finding young in this very spot showed how well informed this egg-collector was.

An RSPB representative was to come to Lewis to help in his detection and by a strange coincidence found himself at Kings Cross Station in the same sleeping compartment as the man he was chasing.

A map of Lewis fell from the bunk above and in the course of subsequent conversation, cleverly manipulated by the man from the RSPB, the egg-collector gave himself away. However, when he stepped off the "Loch Seaforth" at Stornoway and saw his travelling companion of the night before he must have suspected something for we didn't manage to catch him red-handed.

The incident excited my interest in our Lewis green-shanks, but I have not yet succeeded in finding a nest. Every year I come across, here and there, one or two greenshank which display every sign of acute anxiety while I am present. With most species, such behaviour would indicate a nearby nest or young, but I am beginning to believe that greenshank are just made that way.

For example, I put up a greenshank the other day, while traversing one of our less frequented roads, which immediately went into a paroxysm of alarm calls. Since, in my mobile car hide, I was invisible to the bird, it soon began to feed in the flooded moorland by the road. Now and again it would return to the roadside to perch on a peatstack to rest and preen. Sure that it would soon go to its nest to relieve its mate, I waited patiently for almost two hours, scarcely daring to move in case I alarmed the bird. I was close enough to see it blink its white-rimmed eye as it scanned the sky for danger.

My patience, not being of the superhuman kind, possessed by an Eric Hosking or Desmond Nethersole-Thompson, finally was exhausted when the bird showed no sign of a break in its feeding/resting routine. When I returned next day there was no sign of a greenshank and I suspect that, once again, I had encountered an over-excitable greenshank a long way from its nest.

Redshank

Portrait of a Loch

Cradled in a hollow of the hills the Loch lay sleeping under an overcast sky. Behind me rose tier upon tier of craggy gneiss whose tip-tilted wavy bands betrayed ancient earth movements. From the crest of Seabhal opposite, great sheets of heather descended to the lochside, marching with the reseeded area which gleamed with the gold and silver of buttercup and clover like a patch of sunlight.

An islet off-shore bore the ruined broch which gave the Loch its name, among the stones of which Arctic terns once nested. An underwater causeway leads to the broch and sometimes on a hot summer's day I have ventured along it only to lose the way in the peaty water as many a raider must have lost it when the broch was in use and the defenders dependent upon the sinuosity of the causeway for their safety.

A pair of merlins once occupied an old hoodies' nest on a slope above the Loch but, in the manner of merlins, moved on the following year.

The Loch once held excellent brown trout, speckled beauties with rich pink flesh, and it was in pursuit of them one day many years ago that I chanced upon a golden oriole in the heather. Fishing forgotten, I chased this yellow and black exotic from Europe and the Middle East for a second sight of a bird I shall probably never see again and which has not before or since appeared in the Western Isles, in my knowledge.

But today more familiar creatures moved around, several magpie moths had hatched from heather-fed larvae and were making their maiden flights in the still air. When they settled on a lichen covered rock they became almost invisible so effective was their cryptic black, white and orange coloration.

A wren disappeared under an overhanging bunch of heather with a beakful of insects. When I ill-advisedly lifted the heather and peered beneath I almost fell backwards as, one after the other, nine or ten young wrens flew out past my face.

When I had recovered my composure, I watched a pair of ravens sail along the side of Seabhal in the hope that the merlin falcon, if she was still nesting in the vicinity, would sally forth to chase the intruders and thus give away to me her nest-site. Suddenly, there was a great thud to my right. Non-plussed at such a strange sound I looked round to see two ancient ewes squaring up for another head-on collision, encouraged no doubt by a bronchial chorus of appreciation from the rest of the flock.

A splash drew my attention back to the Loch and to the widening circle of ripplets from a rising trout. The insistent notes of a "fidhlear" or common sandpiper flitting along the shore and the calls of a pair of pied wagtails fell gratefully upon my ears as I left this haven of peace.

The Hebridean Orchid

My title may puzzle some folk who think of the orchid as an exotic and beautiful flower grown in this country in hothouses or trailing along the branch of a tree in some East Indian jungle.

It is true that there are some 1500 kinds of orchids, some epiphytic, using a tree for support, some saprophytic, deriving their sustenance from humus on or around a tree and some terrestrial, growing in the ground.

About forty species are native to the United Kingdom, endowed with such strange names as lady's slipper and American lady's tresses. Many are said to resemble the creature whose name they bear: frog, bee, butterfly, spider, fly, lizard and monkey, so versatile are the forms of sepals and petals of the flowers of this talented family, one of the largest in the kingdom of flowers.

The man orchid is said to be in the form of a helmeted man. The lady orchid is described in my *"Pocket Guide to Wild Flowers"* (Collins 1956) as "stately . . . its individual flowers capturing the grace of a lady in Regency flowered chintz crinoline and a purple bonnet!"

The ghost orchid is said to "appear rarely above ground and recorded in nine years only in the past hundred". *(Pocket Guide to Wild Flowers — Collins 1956).*

It is a gratifying fact that we have one member of this extraordinary family of our own, a wine-dark beauty growing in, as far as I know, only one part of Lewis, the Hebridean orchid. A few other orchids are to be found in the machairs of the west, such as the frog, the butterfly and the marsh orchids.

Although less spectacular than some of their relations, these are well worth looking for in June or July in the grassland behind our many shell-sand beaches. The frog and butterfly orchids are by no means conspicuous with their green and white flowers respectively but once found and studied at close quarters their beauty of form and colour and their relationship to their hot-house cousins can be appreciated.

Other species, such as the marsh orchid, prefer more acid conditions and can be found in a great variety of colours on our hills and in our glens.

The Hebridean, frog and butterfly orchids are rare enough to warrant protection and should not be picked but left for others to enjoy.

Crossing the Minch

Some are fast asleep, some deep in gossip, some pale and wretched, longing for a quick death, but a few are bright-eyed and bushy tailed, moving about the deck with binocular or camera at the ready.

The picture is the same whether one is crossing the Minch by "Suilven", "Hebrides", or "Iona", and the voyage passes all too quickly for all but the sea-sick.

There is so much to see on passage whatever the time of year. Apart from the usual satellite gulls, comprising herring and great black-backed gulls and fulmar petrels in winter, there can be seen from time to time common guillemot and razorbill, whose short fast wingbeats distinguish them from the gulls. They are both black above and white below but the former has a pointed bill while the razorbill's is flattened vertically as befits its name.

There is the odd gannet about too, much bigger than the gulls; brilliantly white with black wingtips and yellow heads. Its spectacular dive, unique among sea-birds always seems abortive but the fish is seized and swallowed before the bird surfaces.

Much more can be seen, however, at other seasons of the year. From April onwards, the accompanying gulls may include lesser black-backs together with kittiwakes, while puffins with gaudy bills dive ahead of the ship just before they are engulfed by the wash.

In summer, one might also be lucky enough to spot the dark menacing shape of a great or Arctic skua chasing a gull or tern until, in a panic, the latter disgorges its food which is snapped up by the marauder before it reaches the water.

In late summer, and autumn, Manx shearwaters are beginning to disperse from their breeding slopes on Rhum and are often encountered, skimming gracefully over the waves with rigid, straight wings. Occasionally a rare sooty shearwater, visitor from the south Atlantic may be noticed in their company, its uniform dark colour contrasting with the Manx's white belly.

A large black bird with a six foot wingspan may sometimes be seen winging its way south. This is one of the "gugas" which got away! A young gannet of the year, it will spend the next three years sensibly in warmer latitudes before returning to its breeding ledges in immaculate black and white plumage. Now and again however, a gale will drive a young bird inland.

Just such an unfortunate bird was found loitering in Macaulay Road last autumn by a police constable. Being in possession of a dangerous weapon, by which the intrepid constable was lucky to escape being bitten, it was apprehended and taken into custody. I was called as a defence witness and established its identity and innocence. The bird was subsequently released in Stornoway Harbour, a Niseach nearby being heard to say something about a bird in the hand was worth two on Sula Sgeir.

Secret Places

Tucked away in countless corners in our islands are delectable places which the casual visitor and the sedentary islander will never see.

To their eyes our apparently bleak and monotonous scenery could scarcely contain such charming spots as the mouth of the River Creed in Lewis, Loch Hornary in Grimsay with its wooded islet, typical of so many throughout the Long Island, and the surprising little plantation on the Loch Skipport road in South Uist; and these are only a few examples of the kind of place I mean.

On every visit to South Harris I have been intrigued by a narrow gorge north of the road quite uncharacteristic of the bare stony landscape and on each occasion made a mental note to explore it the next time. Next time eventually came the other day.

A visitor earlier in the summer had reported hearing a ring ousel in the area and the gorge was typical of the haunt of this "mountain blackbird". A summer visitor to Britain, it is about the same size as our blackbird but has a white throat and a much simpler song. As far as I know, there has been no confirmed report of this in the Western Isles so I was disappointed but not altogether surprised not to find one during my walk. My informant could have seen a bird on passage or I could have been looking for a needle in a haystack.

There was, however, ample compensation in other aspects of nature all around.

Unlike the ancient gneiss of most of Lewis, the west side of South Harris is composed of more recent igneous rock. That is, rock which was formed in conditions of great heat and stress within the earth's crust and later extruded. The best known type of igneous rock is granite and one is familiar with the scintillating crystals formed within this rock during the cooling process. Evidence of these formations were all around me as well as long scratches on the surface rock in a NW-SE direction caused by the movement of the great icesheet which covered the Highlands and Islands long ago.

This gorge had probably been cut in softer rock by the action of ice in faults and cracks until running water, during immense periods of time, carved this deep cleft in the native rock. It is thought by some that the builders of the Callanish Stone Circle used this power of ice to obtain the monoliths of which it is composed. Water poured into cracks in winter expanded on freezing with such force as to split great pieces from a cliff-face.

Time and the action of the stream had healed the scar in this instance and the thirty or forty feet high walls of the gorge were clothed with rowan, aspen and alder. The boulders comprising the bed of the stream were rounded and polished by the action of the water in contrast with the rough angular rocks of the adjoining moorland, the sparse vegetation of which compared unfavourably with the riot of colour on any cliff-face exposed to the sun. It was easy to imagine the glen filled with redwing and fieldfare eating their fill of berries, and many other migrant birds looking for shelter, food and water during the autumn gales.

Many insects too find life easier in the sheltered depths of the gorge. Spiders' webs festoon cranny and plant while handsome dragon and damsel flies flit colourfully in the bright sunlight.

The Sound of Barra

Eriskay, Lingay, Fuday, Gighay and Hellisay, all "gude profitable iles perteining to McNeill of Barray", according to Donald Munro in 1549.

They may still be profitable isles to their present owner and they are certainly good to behold, but their main advantages in the present day are the lee they afford and the shelter they give to the creatures of the Sound.

They were particularly enchanting on a recent crossing on a May morning when the sea was glassy calm and a warm sun brought the common seals out on to the skerries, where the shags made heraldic figures with outspread wings drying in the sun.

Every bird within range was easily seen and identifiable and, thanks to our low profile, could be approached more closely than in a bigger vessel. Elegant piebald eider drakes were conspicuous in comparison with their dingy brown mates and the sombre shags and cormorants. There were many flocks of large heavily-built birds, which, shier than the rest, dived afar off.

These were great northern divers, both adults in smart black and white plumage and brown immature birds, which spend the winter on our coasts but breed in the Arctic. Known in Gaelic by the wonderfully evocative name of "murbhuachaill" or "shepherd of the sea", its weird cry causes it to be called the "rain goose" or in America, the common loon.

On the rocky shores of Fuday, small starling-size, tortoise-shell coloured birds probed inconspicuously among the seaweed, industriously turning weed and pebbles over in search of food. Called, not surprisingly therefore, turnstones, these engaging little waders are comparatively tame but are difficult to detect on account of their beautifully cryptic coloration.

Shags

The first Arctic tern is usually seen in the Sound as it works its way north to breed, having spent our winter in the Antarctic. Its pulsating, buoyant flight distinguishes it from the gulls, as does its splashing shallow dives after sand eels. On this occasion a pair of dainty little terns, whose yellow beaks pick them out from their larger red-beaked cousins, could be seen as we neared Eoligarry.

I was still puzzling over the identity of a small mammal which had dived too quickly for me when a voice over my shoulder said "an otter". This was the St. Christopher of the Sound of Barra, Neil Campbell, who has been carrying people like myself across for as long as I can remember and long before that, in all weathers and whose devotion to duty and skill are a byword in these parts.

Like his counterpart in the Sound of Harris, the late John Angus Paterson of Berneray, his uncanny knowledge of these shallow, tide-swept and reef-strewn waters is a revelation to landsmen and a great comfort in time of need.

Owls

One day in May 1972, two visitors told me that they had seen a snowy owl near Barvas in Lewis. This species, native to the Arctic, has turned up from time to time in the Western Isles and has recently bred in the United Kingdom, in Shetland, for the first time.

I had never before seen one myself, so I hastened to the spot and, to my astonishment, for birds rarely wait for me, I saw not just one but two snowy owls. It was a wonderful moment for me when I sat face to face with my first snowy owl, being outstared at a distance of 25 yards with that unscrutable expression unique to this species.

One of them was sitting on a fence post and could scarcely be missed, but fortunately for them they usually prefer to conceal themselves behind a peat bank or beside a white rock, sometimes with just the crown of a snowy white head showing. In fact, I once carefully stalked an abandoned white football from a distance of nearly half a mile, having spotted through the telescope what I thought was a partly concealed owl.

Sadly, these beautiful and useful birds disappeared in the course of the next two years and have not been seen since. Circumstantial evidence points to their having been shot and one person in Barvas is known to have made an attempt; pointless and moronic behaviour by people who should have protected and encouraged such efficient predators of rabbits. Snowy owls have just returned to Shetland, so I hope that a warmer welcome will be extended to any that reach the Western Isles this year.

The only owl resident in any numbers in these Islands is the short-eared owl. Like the snowy owl and the next species, this owl is diurnal, hunting by day, and can be seen in the Uists and Benbecula, rather like a dish-faced buzzard, but with a low rolling flight as it searches for beetles and voles.

It is uncommon in Lewis and Harris, the only occurences being a dead bird found in Bragar in 1954 and one reported recently at Melbost near Stornoway.

The first long-eared owl for the Western Isles was flushed by the writer from an island on Laxavat Ard near Carloway in June, 1956, but this species did not turn up again until 1970 when a boy took home a young owlet from the Stornoway Woods believing it to be an orphan. It proved to be a young long-eared owl and the first to be recorded as having been bred in these Islands. Unfortunately, although it was returned the next day to the place where it had been found, the mother did not succour it and it died. Let us therefore leave any young creature be unless it is in immediate danger or injured; the mother knows best how to care for it.

In 1974, an injured long-eared owl, an adult this time, died of its wounds in Marybank. There have been occasional reports of a tawny owl in the Stornoway Woods, but it has never been proved to breed here. An injured bird, said to be of this species turned up in Ness in 1969, but it too died. An English ornithologist spotted pale-breasted barn owls in Barvas and Benbecula in 1972. This is everyone's idea of the typical owl, nocturnal, ghostly pale and haunting church towers and ruins. It is not difficult to imagine the surprise felt by a householder in Point one morning in February 1973 when she found a barn owl standing near her peat stack, stone dead. It is now in Glasgow Museum, doubtless in more suitable surroundings, with no more worries about surviving a Lewis winter.

Autumn

Migration

No-one who watches birds in autumn even idly, can fail to notice the changes taking place in the kinds of birds around him. On a purely local scale there is movement from moor and woodland to the garden. More robins, tits, thrushes and blackbirds, for instance, are to be seen taking advantage of the shelter and food afforded by garden or croft. Merlins finding the moor deserted by many of the small birds on which they prey are moving into the woods or onto the shore where waders are now so plentiful.

Among these are common sandpipers which have haunted the shore of many a freshwater loch while bringing up a family. Red and black-throated divers and red-breasted mergansers, some still with young, have followed their example and will spend the winter offshore.

Another local migration, peculiar to Stornoway with its extensive woods, is performed by the Lewis ravens which are now to be seen roosting in great numbers in the conifers of Buaile na Cuthaig.

But it is the larger, inter-continental movement of birds which rivets the attention of anyone with eyes to see it. Since the arrival of the first snow buntings, the flood-gates have opened and flocks of redwing and fieldfare have been passing down the Long Island since early October.

The first migrant I myself noted was an immature glaucous gull in Stornoway Harbour on September 27th, which is still with us. The first of our wintering duck from the far north was a long-tailed duck at the Braighe on October 1st to be followed by a pair of scaup and a goldeneye on Loch nan Ràmh. Almost 100 whooper swans were reported at Coll on October 3rd making the welkin ring with their musical chit-chat; smaller parties have been noticed subsequently at Ness, Barvas and Shawbost and doubtless they are by this time arguing with the resident mute swans of the Southern Isles. A woodcock on a Sandwick croft on October 19th must have looked out of place, being more at home in long heather or the rhododendrons of the Castle Grounds.

The rarest migrant to turn up so far this autumn is one of the smallest of the waders, a little stint at Aignish. Only five inches long and a little larger than a robin, this tiny wader from Arctic Russian tundra joins the general southwesterly autumn migration across Europe to the Mediterranean and occasional birds find their way to our shores.

Although we all know that our swallows and martins spend the winter in Africa instead of in the mud of a pool, as our forefathers believed, no one really knows how they manage to navigate over these vast distances and somehow I find comfort in the knowledge that there is still something left in the world beyond our under-standing.

Waxwings

One Sunday I happened to notice a neighbour waving to me from his window. "How nice" I thought and waved genially back. It wasn't until a day or two later that we met and he asked me if I had seen the waxwing in my garden which he had indicated to me on the Sunday. That bird proved to be one of the few waxwings to be seen in Stornoway that autumn and I had missed it in my own garden.

Some years there is, however, a positive outbreak of waxwings, and I can remember counting twenty within six feet of my bedroom window. Two years running a waxwing turned up in Shawbost and I have come across them from Ness to Tarbert.

According to the records I have kept for the past number of years, we in the Western Isles may expect to see waxwings from October to December but few in the spring.

It seems that if there are too many waxwings in Finland and Northern Russia, where they breed, for the wild berries available, a greater or lesser number migrate in search of food in proportion to the amount of food available.

Bad summers give us more waxwings presumably. Many birds are caught by easterly winds and find themselves in the British Isles and those from northern Finland and Russia find little to satisfy them in Shetland and Orkney and press on until they reach us.

Many gardens possess such berry-bearing bushes as cotoneaster and honeysuckle which the native blackbirds, thrushes and wandering redwing have spurned and which, unlike our rowans, still bear a heavy crop of little berries.

Somehow, the waxwings find these, wherever they are in the Island, strip them bare in a very short time and depart. It is worth anyone's while spending a few moments watching these interesting birds for they are quite tame and very beautiful. A little smaller than a starling but plumper and a rich brown in colour, they possess a conspicuous, swept-back crest, bright yellow edges to tail and wing and scarlet, wax-like tips to some of the wing feathers, which gives the species its name. A grey rump and black through the eye and under the chin complete a striking plumage which once seen is never forgotten.

Mention should also be made of the musical call which, here at any rate, does not accord with its Latin name, Bombycilla garrulus, but which often brings our attention to their presence.

Long-tailed duck

More Migrants

One stormy evening in October, 1970, I had a telephone call from a householder in Northton to say that his garden was swarming with brent geese. Since I had seen this rather rare species but twice before in these islands and then only in ones and twos, I had naturally assumed that it was an infrequent visitor. This report, however, showed that huge flocks probably pass through the Hebrides every autumn — but unseen by night. The house concerned stands up prominently in the low ground between the South Harris hills and Toe Head and the 150 geese, flying low down the west coast under the storm, collided with the houses and outbuildings.

This west coast flyway is used every autumn by several other species of geese and duck and on a clear night, if one listens carefully, it is often possible to hear them talking to each other as they make their way south; sometimes the high-pitched yapping of pinkfoot or whitefront or the deeper clangorous honking of greylag.

If headed by adverse winds, they will rest on the Uist machair or on the Lewis reseeded moorland. Those which have been drifted eastwards are sometimes found in Broadbay together with hundreds of wintering wigeon.

Many other species of duck visit us at this time of year, although in smaller numbers than the wigeon, and one of the best places in Lewis to watch them is the little loch at the Braighe and on the sea there. I should think I have seen fifteen different kinds of duck there.

One of the most attractive and more numerous of these is the long-tailed duck. Smaller than a mallard and with very variable brown and white plumage, the long-tailed breeds in the Arctic and winters in the coastal waters of northern Europe. The drake's winter plumage is almost entirely white but for a dark patch on the side of the head and he, only, sports a long slender tail. Their loud musical call is quite unmistakable and one of the delights of winter bird-watching. They are also, like most of the other sea and diving ducks on the Braighe which feed on shellfish, inedible.

The Greylag Goose

The greylag is generally regarded as the harbinger of changing seasons and it is therefore appropriate in September to look at this bird more closely. The progenitor of the domestic, farmyard goose, which it resembles, the greylag is our only native breeding goose.

Once widespread throughout the Western Isles it has suffered continuous harrassment, both by shooting and by theft of the eggs, until it is now confined to Loch Druidebeg in South Uist and a few isolated pairs on offshore islands. It should, perhaps, be noted by some folk that the greylag is protected and may not be shot or its eggs taken between the 1st of February and the 31st of August.

Apart from small colonies in the Northern counties of Scotland, the Western Isles are in fact now the main stronghold of the greylag so that the Nature Conservancy-managed Reserve in South Uist is a very important factor in its survival.

Even during my twenty-eight years in Lewis, I have seen this shy bird driven from its breeding grounds on the west side by heather burning and egg-stealing to the point of extinction, thus depriving our dwindling natural environment of another wild creature. It sometimes seems to me that the present generation is bent on the extermination of as many of these creatures as possible and one doesn't need to look further than the herring, the salmon and the golden eagle for examples. So I look to the youngsters of today for a saner attitude to wildlife and to their teachers for its inculcation.

On the continent, the greylag is the most abundant of the thirteen species of geese and every autumn great flocks come winging in from the Atlantic en route to their wintering grounds in the south. Flying in loose, straggling arrowheads behind the leader, a formation which allows each goose both to avoid the slipstream of the bird ahead and to see where it is going, the geese communicate with a deep, sonorous "aahng-ung-ung", so familiar in the farmyard and so different from the cackle of the bird when disturbed.

Anyone who has trespassed on the territory of a domestic flock will understand the feelings of the intrepid Gaul who, silently scaling the Capitoline Hill of Rome in 390 BC, startled the sacred geese and alerted the garrison thus saving the city and earning an honoured place in its annals for the goose.

The greylag is a large bird of thirty-two inches in length and five foot wingspan with an orange bill and white tail terminating in a dark bank. They pair for life and produce four to six young each year after some twelve weeks incubation and fledging. The origin of the name is not known but is probably derived from the old word meaning late.

Snow Buntings

One of my bird books describes snow buntings as "Snow Flakes", and my immediate impression when I happened upon nine of them at the Butt of Lewis was certainly of large flakes of snow rising and falling against the bleak autumnal landscape.

I have never seen snow buntings in their black and white breeding plumage worn in Iceland, Greenland and Northern Scandinavia. By the time they reach Lewis in autumn on migration they have moulted and brown and grey have replaced the black mantle and tail. From October onwards through the winter snow buntings may be seen on the shore or by the roadside. Their cryptic coloration renders them almost invisible until they take flight, when their shimmering beauty takes one's breath away.

There are said to be 522 species of buntings in the world but only twelve occur in the United Kingdom and, of these, only nine have been reported in the Western Isles. The red-headed bunting, which turns up now and again, is usually disregarded as an escaped cage-bird — I saw one in South Uist last year. The best known bunting is the yellowhammer which is practically unknown in the Western Isles but is a familiar bird of the hedgerow on the mainland with its peculiar, wheezy song rendered in English as "A little bit of bread and no che-ese".

I have the impression that our own commonest bunting

has become less comon in Lewis. Formerly, one could hear the corn bunting's jingling call from fence and telephone wire almost anywhere from Stornoway to Ness but now I seem to come across only the odd one in Back and Ness. In the Southern Isles it is still as common as ever. The dapper reed bunting can be found in most reed beds, clinging sturdily to waving reeds as he stutters and stammers in a vain effort to produce a song.

The snow bunting, on the other hand, has a musical, rippling twitter, only a suggestion of which, unfortunately, we hear from our winter visitors. In the Cairngorms, its most southerly breeding ground, only a few pairs nest, mainly above 3,000 feet. A nest and eggs were once found on St. Kilda in 1913 but we must wait, I'm afraid, for another similar cold spell before looking for a nesting "bigean sneachda" (little bird of the snow?) on the Clisham or Hecla.

The Isle of Barra

One of the putative derivations of the name Barra is the old Norse "Bar-ey", the bare island. This may well have been an apt description a thousand years ago when the Vikings overran the Hebrides and found treeless, round-shouldered Barra bare in comparison with their forest-clad, mountainous homeland.

Today, to someone from Lewis in particular, Barra is anything but bare. In fact, the description of England Shakespeare puts in the mouth of John of Gaunt always comes to my mind on a visit to Barra, especially if the sun is shining as it nearly always is on my all too infrequent visits . . . "this scepter'd isle . . . this precious stone set in the silver sea . . ."

During one twenty-four hour stay one autumn on the island, most of which were spent safe-guarding the Nation's revenue or asleep (the two activities are not compatible), I noted thirty-eight species of birds. All of these were those I would have expected to find, like the first I saw as I stepped from the aircraft, a buzzard quartering the sand dunes at the Cockle Strand. But a blackcap at Brevig was a bonus and a correspondent

who had spent a holiday in Barra a few weeks earlier had seen some unexpected birds, such as moorhens at Borve and Northbay, where he had seen also a green sandpiper, pied and spotted flycatchers, a linnet and a redpoll.

Most of the time I had was spent in the little groups of trees at the Glen in Castlebay, the sycamores at Brevig and the mixed wood at Northbay, all of which I had, perforce, passed by on previous visits. Who I wondered, had planted these trees and when? Those at Northbay, comprising at least thirteen different kinds of trees and shrubs, provide wonderful cover for migrants and resident insect-eating birds, such as warblers.

I was therefore not surprised to find a small colony of goldcrest. As I stood motionless at the edge of the wood several of these tiny olive-green birds with brilliant gold and scarlet crests came in turn within a few feet of me as they fed along the glossy green spruce branches.

It was a surprise however to find thriving specimens of sweet chestnut, maple and a small tree I took to be Portugal laurel. There is such substantial shelter in this wood now that many more interesting shrubs and flowers could be grown successfully and enjoyed by islanders and visitors alike if a path were constructed along the bank of the stream through the middle of the wood, from which the many birds which must use its shelter could be more easily observed.

Sick Birds

"Are not two sparrows sold for a farthing? and not one of them shall not fall on the ground without your Father". (Matthew 10:29)

Most people feel rather helpless when encountering a sick or injured bird where there is no outward evidence of the cause.

It was to help anyone in such a quandary that the Royal Society for the Protection of Birds brought out a little booklet entitled *"Treatment of Sick and Injured Birds"* which may be obtained from the Society at the Lodge,

Sandy, Bedfordshire, SG19 2DL, for the cost of a stamped, self-addressed envelope.

Generally, whatever is wrong with the bird it will benefit from a rest in darkness at first and this can best be provided in a box or carton of suitable size, well ventilated and provided with a layer of straw or similar material. If the bird is temporarily incapacitated by concussion caused, for example, by hitting a window or overhead wire or car it will recover in a few hours sufficiently to permit release.

If there is no sign of injury and the bird allows itself to be picked up and does not recover after a rest it is probably beyond help and should be humanely killed. In the absence of professional assistance this is best done by a sharp blow on the back of the head. This is not a course which will appeal to many people, but the alternative of allowing the bird to die a slow death is really more cruel.

Some diseases of birds are transmissible to man and most birds carry parasites so care should always be taken to wash after handling birds.

A convalescent bird must eventually be fed and food appropriate to the species should be used. Bread should be given only in an emergency. Robins, thrushes, and other thin-billed birds require insects, thick-billed birds such as sparrows and finches will take seed and larger birds, such as crows and gulls will often eat any scraps. Birds of prey need red meat, preferably with fur or skin attached. All birds benefit from water either for drinking or washing.

When the time comes to release the patient it should be taken to the kind of place familiar to it, if it is impracticable to return it to the spot where found. Oiled seabirds may be dusted gently with Fuller's earth until the oil has been removed. It is important to remember in this connection that the bird must be dried properly and kept in a warm place because most of the natural waterproofing properties of the plumage will have been removed with the oil and the bird must be given time to replace it by preening.

Young birds, whose parents may be absent finding food for them, are often thought to be sick and are picked up by misguided persons who have little idea of the problem involved in feeding them.

Only where it is confirmed by a return visit that the fledgling has been abandoned and is not being fed should it be removed. The booklet gives detailed advice as to treatment of such creatures.

Racing pigeons, carried off course by easterly winds, often land here weak and hungry. They may be recognised by their tameness and the rings on their legs and should be left alone to rest and feed until sufficiently recovered to resume their flight to their owner's loft where they will get no prizes but will doubtless tell their fellows what a wonderful holiday they had in the islands!

Great Northern Diver

The Butt of Lewis

A low pressure area between Greenland and Iceland was producing a great sweep of westerly winds across the North Atlantic. Perhaps the redwing and geese which visit us each autumn from these islands, having been thwarted for so long by adverse winds, would now be able to make the long passage to our western shores. So off I went to their probable landfall, the Butt of Lewis.

Not only did I see several weary redwing flopping from one sheltered ditch to another but also two dapper wheatears feeding busily on tiny insects, having just landed en route to their winter home in Africa. It was while looking for these gallant little migrants that I noticed some commotion in the water below the light-house. This area is seldom calm, being the meeting place of tide and wind, but it now resembled a maelstrom as twenty to thirty dolphins had a whale of a time. Battening probably on the rich feeding thrown up by the turbulent seas, they twisted and turned at incredible speed as they fought for food. Many jumped clear of the water in the excitement, or perhaps for the joy of living.

From my elevated view-point I could follow them under water until they surfaced again, especially if one turned on its back and showed its white belly through the limpid water. Knowing thus when a dolphin was about to surface I could watch for the characteristic protruding beak and the blow-hole opening and closing as it inhaled. Their breathing was both audible and visible in the faint spray of moisture in the exhalation.

What a setting for such accomplished display! On one side are the strikingly intricate inverted folds of rock exposed by the action of the sea, evidence of the gigantic forces loosed long ago by nature during the cooling of the earth's crust, and beyond, the immensity of the ocean.

If one could travel due north from the Butt of Lewis to the Pole and over the top, the first landfall would be the coast of eastern Siberia, nearly 4,000 miles distant. Due west there would be no landfall for 2,250 miles until one reached Hebron in Labrador. Alas, where are the men of war with a perfect heart to make a David king in this Hebron?

Winter

Great Northern

Almost as big as a goose, the great northern diver, (Gavia immer) is also known as the common loon, though the last might be a misleading nickname in the Broch. Sometimes known as the rain-goose, its call is supposed to presage rain.

Axel Munthe, the Swedish author of "The Story of San Michele", describes the Laplander's version of this diver's weird bad-weather call as "Var luk, var luk, luk, luk". That inveterate collector of names and sounds of nature, A.R. Forbes, attributes it to the black-throated diver and renders the Gaelic form as "Deoch, deoch, deoch'san loch a' tràghadh".

Although the great northern diver is not uncommon around our coasts six months of the year, while escaping from the Icelandic winter, I have never heard it calling. Possibly, in view of our winter climate, the bird loses its voice soon after arrival or realises that it is wasting its time forecasting rain.

Until 1970, the great northern diver was not known to breed in this country, its breeding grounds being confined to Iceland, Greenland and North America, but in that year a pair reared young on a loch in Wester Ross and the following year a hybrid great northern/black-throated diver bred with a black-throated diver on the same loch.

It is therefore interesting to re-read that enchanting book, "Great Northern?" which Arthur Ransome published in 1947 and in which he recounts the fictional adventures of a group of children and their efforts to protect the eggs of a pair of great northern divers supposed to have been found in Lewis. It is sad to reflect that human nature has probably changed as little as the Lewis landscape in the intervening years and such rare eggs coveted just as ardently now as in 1947.

The great northern diver has an even rarer cousin, the white-billed diver, (Gavia adamsii) named after a Mr Adams who could not have been so egotistical as the George Steller after whom the famous Steller's eider of South Uist is named, or perhaps, he didn't relish the possibility of being known to posterity by the name "Adam's loon!"

Only twenty or so of these rare vagrants from the high Arctic have been sighted in this country but none so far confirmed in the Western Isles.

I myself am convinced that I saw one in Loch Carloway in 1961 and on 3rd January 1977 watched a diver in Stornoway harbour in nondescript winter plumage with a light coloured, tip-tilted beak and faint barrings on its back which could have been a white-billed diver.

I cannot be sure, however, and must be resigned, as happens so often in bird-watching, (and a useful mortification it is) to suffixing the record with a question mark rather than indulge in wishful thinking. But it did look so awfully like a white-billed diver.

Feeding Garden Birds

Many people who have gardens find themselves interested in the birds which visit them and are noting that more are to be seen now than during the summer. This is because food is becoming scarcer in the wild, while many gardens still have bushes loaded with berries and, as far as mine is concerned anyway, an inexhaustible supply of slugs, snails and weed-seeds. It must be said, however, that there has been a notice-able decline in the former since a slow-worm was released in the garden some time ago and I hope he wakes up after his hibernation in time to regain control.

The more familiar birds like robin, thrush and blackbird are the main immigrants from the surrounding country-side while in Stornoway gardens, blue and great tits are also becoming an almost daily occurrence from now on. One may see too, wrens, pied wagtails, redpoll, chaffinch, greenfinch and dunnock or hedge sparrow. Starling and house sparrow are of course never far away when there is food around. A rose-coloured starling, a rare vagrant from eastern Europe and possibly the only one in the U.K. at the time, came to a Tarbert garden last summer with common starlings just because they were in the habit of finding food there.

In the harder weather of December and January, these species can easily become dependent on what we put out for them in our gardens, especially in times of hard frost when a supply of water is essential for survival. There are, therefore, certain ways of keeping our garden birds alive in return for the service they render in decimating insect pests. A fresh supply of tepid water in the morning after frost is a first requirement.

Secondly, a bird table at a sufficient height to protect the birds from the all too common stray cats around, sheltered by a roof to keep off the omnivorous gulls and, if possible, in a sheltered part of the garden where it can be watched from the house without disturbing the feeding birds.

Different species require different food. Tits will enjoy shelled peanut (if you can find any) in a suitable container to which they can cling in their own inimitable manner. A delicacy which will draw them from far and near is easily made by melting a little fat, together with currants, raisins, etc, in a cream carton in which a string is placed. When the fat has solidified it may be removed from the carton and suspended below the bird-table or from the branch of a tree or high bush out of the range of cats. A lump of suet or a half coconut shell can be hung in the same way.

There are proprietary mixtures of wild bird food available which are ideal for spreading on the bird-table, together with edible kitchen scraps, fruit, bones, etc. It must be emphasised however, that such exotic food should be withdrawn in the spring before nestlings can be fed with it.

The table and receptacles for both food and water should of course, be kept scrupulously clean and the food renewed regularly.

Gulls

Winter is a good time of year to discuss this large family for not only are they more easily observed and identified but some of their exotic cousins may be found wintering with them.

In spring and summer, the breeding birds are scattered over the Western Isles. Lewis seems to specialise in inland colonies on the moor while the gulls of the Southern Isles prefer the small offshore islands, but everywhere they are to be found also in coastal cliffs and fresh water islands. In winter, however, and especially in fishing ports such as Stornoway, the entire population seems to be concentrated in the harbour and it is usually possible to see three or four species.

The most common is, of course, the herring gull which in adult plumage of snowy white breast and head and

Pied wagtail

pearly grey mantle is really quite a handsome bird. The immature herring gull wears his nondescript brown and white for three years and is difficult to distinguish from his coeval cousin, the great black-backed gull except by smaller size, being some four inches shorter and less heavily built.

The adult great black-backed gull is conspicuous by his size and black wings and deeper voice, a sound the trout fisherman learns to loathe if he upsets a breeding pair.

The next most common member of the family is the black-headed gull which paradoxically doesn't have a black head at this time of year, but it is a much smaller and daintier bird, whose beak and legs are dark red, whereas those already mentioned have flesh-coloured legs and yellow beaks with a red spot on the lower mandible. The young of this species have a beautiful black and white phase.

In Stornoway we can nearly always be sure of seeing an Iceland gull or a glaucous gull from Greenland and Iceland respectively — and I haven't got it the wrong way round! They can both be recognised by the absence of black wing tips which makes them conspicuously lighter in appearance than the herring or black-backed gull.

It is usually young birds we get here which take four or five years to reach maturity, sometimes turning pure white in the process, when they may be confused with an albino herring gull. An adult glaucous gull has turned up at the Braighe in recent years and young ones have been seen in Tarbert, Ness and Benbecula.

A rare ivory gull was seen in Stornoway in November, 1961 and a little gull in South Uist in July, 1969. There is no doubt that other rare gulls visit the Western Isles in winter and escape recognition. Any unusual gull should therefore be reported to someone who can ensure that it is identified and recorded.

Rooks and Jackdaws

Having received reports of rooks and jackdaws in South Uist and Benbecula in 1975 and having myself seen small flocks of both on Benbecula aerodrome in April 1976, I was not altogether surprised to read in the "Stornoway Gazette" in December 1976 that these birds had been seen again. They were said to have turned up on the west side of the island; so, on a visit on 9th December, I verified that they were not in fact on the aerodrome and proceeded to keep an eye open for them on the way to South Uist.

Now rooks and jackdaws are about the blackest birds we have and comparatively easy to pick out on a reasonable day. But this was not a reasonable day. The light was so poor in and between blinding showers of hail and sleet that all birds appeared black and binoculars were useless to eyes watering in the icy wind.

Many of the fresh-water lochs were sealed with a skin of ice thick enough to make them useless to most wildfowl which had, presumably, sought refuge in the sea. Some curlew and redshank probed the machair for the few worms foolish enough to venture near the surface and small flocks of twite flitted from field to field in search of what seed the winnowing wind had left. Duck huddled close under the banks in pockets of open water and even Loch Mór seemed bereft of birds.

A solitary redwing, almost twice its normal size with feathers fluffed out to retain its body heat, pecked hopelessly by the roadside. But no rooks or jackdaws. A hooded crow now and again raised my hopes until its grey waistcoat revealed its identity.

The return journey was made in sunlight however, and when on the outskirts of Balivanich, I noticed a flock of restless black birds in a field I stopped to examine them closely and was delighted to find that it was a mixed flock of rooks and jackdaws. There were many more of the latter than last year.

In the stinging wind, it was difficult to count them as they fed greedily among the long grass, but I reckon that there were about twenty of each species.

Many will now be familiar with these birds for their occurrence in Benbecula is, I think, a rare phenomenon. The rook is the larger of the two and is completely blue-black except for a bare patch between beak and eyes. The jackdaw is distinguished by his bright eye and grey head. Both are beneficial, unless in excessive numbers, consuming large numbers of the more reprehensible insects, like leatherjackets. Both species breed in the Western Isles but are confined to Stornoway, whither they came in the autumn of 1893 from the continent.

It would seem reasonable to assume that our present migrants came from the nearest colonies on Skye but it may be that they are still following in the wake — I nearly wrote "footsteps" — of these earlier adventurers.

Storks

Anyone in the Western Isles coming across a very large, black, heron-like bird with a seven inch red beak and long red legs might be excused for "taking the pledge" or seeing an optician. But in fact, a Mr J.O.B. Rossetti had just such an experience on August 30th, 1974 while walking over Vallay Strand in North Uist.

This record of a black stork, the third in Scotland, has been accepted and lends colour to a report of a similar bird seen in Camus Uig in Lewis.

There are two kinds of stork found in Europe, both of which could occur in these islands; these are the white and black storks.

The former is the gregarious, chimney-top nester of popular paedotrophic reputation, to which the arrival of a baby in a Victorian family was attributed. Despite its usefulness as a scapegoat and as a scavenger, which has led to its protection in Europe, the white stork, formerly plentiful in Britain, has largely disappeared from Western Europe. Apart from some 24,000 pairs in Spain and Portugal, the main breeding grounds are now in eastern Europe, Asia Minor and North Africa. The black stork has retreated even further into Russia.

The latter is a solitary bird and inordinately shy. Its handsome black plumage, irridescent with purple and green, long red legs and dagger-like bill, distinguish it from any other bird.

Storks are soaring birds, like eagles and buzzards, possessing broad wings capable of lifting their 7 lb.

owner, in migration to and from Africa, high enough in thermals, columns of warm rising air, to cross the Straits of Gibralter, the Bosporus and, even, the central Mediterranean by way of Tunisia and Malta.

Unlike its relation, the heron, which deceives its prey by complete immobility and last minute lightning strike, the stork stalks the marsh or the shallow waters of a lagoon until it sights its prey, which it surprises with a short run of two or three steps and envelopes in shade with outstretched wings.

The normal food of this stork comprises frogs and salamanders, neither of which will keep a stork alive for very long in the Outer Hebrides.

A Sparrowhawk

There is a grove of trees in Uig which I have long wanted to visit. It was planted probably about 120 years ago by Sir James Matheson and therefore I should not have been surprised at the variety of trees when I eventually had a look at it. Besides the usual Corsican pine, rowan and sycamore, there were ash, beech, birch, holly, laburnum and Norway maple.

A sparrowhawk had been reported in the vicinity of these trees and I hoped to see it, being a woodland bird, the sparrowhawk is very rare in these islands. In fact there are only about twenty records and since breeding, although suspected in Lewis, has never been proved, these records may all be of vagrant birds. The Castle Grounds provide the only really suitable environ-ment for this species and may well conceal a pair. In April 1976 I watched a pair of unfamiliar predators soaring above Strawberry Hill which I tried to persuade myself were sparrowhawks.

I ransacked the Uig wood without success and was retiring reluctantly when I noticed a commotion above the trees. My binocular revealed a dog-fight between a merlin falcon and two hooded crows: at least it looked like a dog-fight at first, but when I saw the crows retaliating and neither party giving up I began to wonder if they were not just enjoying a friendly contest. I have seldom seen such a brilliant and sustained exhibition of flying skill when the little falcon stooped with half-closed wings at an incredible speed as each crow in turn towered heavenwards to renew the attack. The crows cleverly evaded each stoop with a half-roll and now and again almost caught the merlin at a disadvantage at the bottom of her dive. The crows could easily have escaped at any time but, as I say, I got the impression that they were enjoying a game and I believe birds are not always credited with the sense of fun they seem to possess.

Soon, however, a fourth contender appeared on the scene, a slightly larger bird of prey with a slate-grey back and reddish breast. But it was the longish barred tail and rounded wings which told me that the sparrowhawk had arrived. This was too much for the crows which disappeared. Then followed an even more exciting display of flying as the merlin chased the hawk through the trees at breakneck speed. The latter occasionally tried to perch and rest but one or two dives by the falcon soon dislodged him. Twice the merlin swept off over an adjacent hill; twice the sparrowhawk began to hunt outwards from the wood but the merlin must have been waiting off-stage and twice she returned to chase the larger bird back into the wood whence, at the end, he failed to reappear.

Mammals and Other Creatures

Frogs and Toads

One of these incidents occurred the other day, similar to the kind which often sparks off a Nature Note. A friend brought me a creature in the hope that I might be able to identify it. Such faith is touching and I was glad to be able to say without doubt that it was a common toad: common that is in the United Kingdom but the first of which I have knowledge for the Western Isles.

It is popularly supposed, in fact, that there are no amphibians, that is, frogs, toads, newts, etc. in these islands. St. Columba, it seems, banished them from Ireland but there is no record whose displeasure the amphibians of the Western Isles incurred. There have been frequent attempts within my knowledge to introduce frogs to Lewis. These seemed to have failed, possibly because our standing water is too acid for them. This, as all folk who have been working with peat recently will agree, is a pity for their favourite food is midge larvae.

In October 1962, I was given a frog found in the grounds of Lewis Hospital. It was released in my garden pool but was never seen again.

It must be assumed that the toad referred to above was introduced to this island for it was found in the middle of the road on the West Side on August 11th. Apart from anything else it will be interesting to know how far it had travelled and in what direction. The creature is now in the care of the Nicolson Institute.

Shakespeare called the toad ugly and venomous. To the Israelites, frogs were pestilential and John, in his Revelation, saw them as foul spirits.

I dare say few people would admit to an affection for frogs or toads or bemoan their absence from these islands, but I believe that to some folk they are engaging creatures and they are certainly worthy of note, not least for the recapitulation they display in their growth from tadpoles of their evolution from fishes. The former possess, for example, fish-like tails and external gills which in the adult have disappeared, the gills becoming lungs.

The third species I have referred to is the newt, which again so far as I am aware, does not occur in these islands. Someone who is not normally given to imposing on my credulity, once found a newt in a matchbox in Goathill Road. This is neither the condition nor the place in which one would expect to find a newt and its status must be regarded with some doubt.

To close, may I appeal to anyone who has seen or heard a grasshopper or cricket in the Western Isles to get in touch with me.

Sticklebacks

A fish which glows red when courting, builds a nest and looks after his off-spring single-handed, so to speak. One of these queer tropical creatures, no doubt, you think. But no, am biorag-lodain can be found not much more than a stone's throw from your house. He comes in two varieties, three and fifteen-spined.

The three-spined is the smaller, only a couple of inches long in the islands, and lives in our lochs and estuaries. The fifteen-spined is more than twice as long, lives in the sea and can scarcely be recognised as a relation of the former. It should perhaps be mentioned, that there is a third species with ten spines which is unlikely to be met with here.

When the three-spined stickleback assumes his reddish spawning dress in the spring he builds a nest of weed and grass about the size of a fist, binding the material with an excretion from his kidney and anchoring the nest to the bottom. The nest has one hole into which he lures an amenable mate and keeps her there until she has laid her eggs and chewed her way out the opposite side, to play no further part in the proceedings.

The male stations himself at one hole and, after fertilizing the eggs, maintains a continuous circulation of water over them with his fins until they hatch, when he opens out the nest into a sort of cradle. Until the young fish become independent he will act in a most pugnacious manner to any aggressor or predator many times his own size. He has been known to attack even an inanimate red object, an instinctive reaction to the red coloration of another stickleback.

Little information is available on the distribution of these two species in the Western Isles. Correspondents have stated that the three-spined are to be found in the following lochs in Lewis and in the Broadbay area: Stiapavat, Orosay, Garry, and also in Garynahine and Grimersta estuaries. But there must be many other lochs and streams where they occur in the Long Island and I shall welcome positive information relating to each species.

Otters

Fishing a loch near Carloway on a September day some years ago, I became conscious of a high pitched call behind me. It was not like the call of any bird I knew and eventually my curiosity got the better of my lust for salmon.

Placing my fly-rod on the bank I carefully made my way towards a heathery knoll whence the noise came. At first nothing could be seen, then suddenly I was astonished to see two young otters running nose to tail round a rock at the water's edge not ten yards from me.

I was at a loss to account for their odd behaviour until I caught sight of an adult otter swimming towards the youngsters from an island some twenty-five yards off-shore. She spotted me simultaneously, as so often happens when one looks directly into the eye of a wild creature, and hesitated momentarily. The maternal instinct took over, however, and she carried on to the shore, plucked up one of the young by the scruff of the neck and returned to the island.

I took advantage of her back being turned and crept to within a yard of the remaining pup to see what would happen next. He continued to run, calling, round the rock while the mother dropped her burden on the island and swam back towards me, ignorant of the fact that she was being followed by the first pup!

Regardless of my conspicuous presence she lifted the second pup from beneath my feet and headed once

again for the island, still followed by the other pup. My last sight of them before taking up my rod again was of the whole family reunited on the island, including the father who had materialised during the episode.

I have enjoyed many other encounters with this delightful, intelligent and interesting species but never at such close quarters.

They are relatively common in the Western Isles at present but were once almost wiped out by game-keepers on account of their skins. One keeper boasted of having killed 78 in his 25 years as a keeper. An increasing threat to their survival has turned up in the form of the feral mink, which, like the otter, feeds mainly on fish, small birds and mammals. The mink, however, is aggressive and bloodthirsty and could displace the gentle and playful otter from its formerly undisputed niche in the wild. This would be a great pity and an illustration of what can happen when an alien species is introduced.

The male otter is much larger than a mink, being from three to four feet long and weighing up to 30 lbs. While the mink is variable in colour, the otter is uniformly brown. Both species are amphibious and have webbed feet enabling them with the aid of a powerful tail to overtake even salmon.

The otter, I am happy as an angler to say, is much more beneficial than the mink as he eats many eels. Most of the year is spent by the sea, coming up the rivers only in summer to prey on fresh water fish. It is then that they are most often seen.

I have followed an otter up a spawning stream with scarcely enough water to cover him and I have lain motionless on a clifftop near Breanish, watching an otter apparently ignorant of my presence pass a few paces from me and disappear down a gully.

Changing Fortune

I remember one fishing season when most fishing bags had been pretty empty on the way home, and mine more than most. My credibility as an angler was becoming suspect, my self-confidence was being sapped and I was beginning seriously to contemplate a more productive pastime, such as marbles. However, in the face of adverse easterly winds and exceptionally low water conditions, I and a friend decided to follow a hunch and try once again. Two days before I had risen a couple of salmon without hooking them in my usual inimitable manner, refraining from "striking" with exemplary restraint until the fish pulled first — which of course they did not. All my pre-conceived ideas, plausible theories culled from all the best books on how to catch salmon, and advice from people who had actually caught salmon were proving to be, like trial by jury according to an 18th century Lord Chief Justice, "a delusion, a mockery, and a snare". "Sheer unrewarded toil", Lord Grey of Falloden called it.

When fishing for trout it is accepted that the speed of the strike is the secret of success and the quickness of the hand deceives the trout. Were the two species so different, I was beginning to wonder, that salmon could not similarly be deceived? "Facilis descensus Averni" — the road to evil is easy! But I was saved in the nick of time by this latest outing when, within five minutes of starting, a salmon leaped out of the water to take the fly. This was a new gambit and proved mutually advantageous because we got our excitement and the fish its eventual freedom, being lightly hooked by its precipitous behaviour.

The next fish was really unlucky, for rising obviously to the first fly and, true to form, missing, it was hooked in the back by the following tail fly. Such carelessness brought its own punishment and eventual demise in the bottom of the boat. But I was fairly cured of my near apostasy by the next two fish which allowed me to experience for only the second time this season the supreme satisfaction of hooking a salmon on the fly. There is nothing quite like it and even the excitement and tension of playing a fish tends to be somewhat of an anti-climax. To be able to persuade a creature of many pounds weight, some four or five years old, which has survived a double journey across the Atlantic, to take a bunch of feathers of one's own tying into its mouth, is no mean feat and then to pit one's skill against that of the fish, linked by a slender line, whose breaking strain is little more than the weight of the fish.

Small wonder that so many baskets are empty!

A Sowerby's Whale on Gress Sands

The mesoplodons, or beaked whales are a small group distinguished by a long beak, of which little is known and I would have been willing, until recently, to accept a reasonable wager that they would not figure in one of my Notes. In the Lews, however, anything can happen and I really should not have been surprised to find a beaked whale on Gress Sands on 5th January 1977, when following up a report of a stranded dolphin.

It was fifteen feet long with a black back, whitish belly flecked with black and could have been confused with a dolphin except for its size and the dorsal fin which was set much further back than a dolphin's. The snout or beak, twelve inches long, was longer, too, than a dolphin's.

What puzzled me on my first examination was the fact that the creature seemed to have no teeth and I surmised that here was something out of the ordinary. Unfortunately, someone had foolishly cut out two or three square feet of blubber from the back ruining the carcase as a potential museum specimen.

As Receiver of Wreck for the Western Isles, I have access to a handy little book published by the British Museum on British whales to assist me in identifying Royal Fish.

Now, in England, Wales and Northern Ireland, all whales, porpoises, dolphins and sturgeons are Royal Fish and belong to the Crown when stranded on a Crown foreshore, which comprises most of our shore-line except for small sections owned by private persons. Perhaps, since strandings of the smaller whales are more common in Scotland, only whales of more than twenty-five feet are Royal Fish and come under my protection. The snag, from my point of view, is that I am also responsible for disposing of unwanted Royal Fish and, in my experience, it is not easy to dispose of an eighty foot blue whale by telephone.

Referring, as I say, to my book, I reached the opinion that this little fellow was a beaked whale and possibly a True's beaked whale, which is so rare that there was only an outline of the creature in the book and which had been stranded only three times in British waters since records began in 1913 until 1966.

In view of its apparent rarity, the British Museum was informed and I subsequently received a request for the lower jaw and to secure the whale if possible. It transpired that it could be one of two species: True's beaked whale which has a tooth in the tip of the lower jaw or a Sowerby's whale whose tooth is halfway down its jaw.

With the gallant help of a colleague, I severed the lower jaw, thanking my lucky stars as I washed the blood off the saw, that I had resisted parental pressure to enter the medical profession and that it was fish for tea.

I was later advised by the Museum that my specimen was a Sowerby's whale and the mystery of the missing tooth was cleared up. It was a female whose tooth is hidden in the gum. One can only assume that the male of the species is a docile creature when his mate doesn't need to show her teeth!

Hares

My interest has been aroused by recent reports of hares being seen again in Lewis. It is many years since I last saw one and I was afraid that they had gone forever.

We are referring, of course, to the blue or mountain hare (gearra-gheal or maigheach-gheal) which is said to have been introduced into Harris during the 19th century and to have spread into Lewis in such numbers that hare drives over the Barvas moor are possibly still within living memory. It is reputed to be absent from Benbecula, South Uist and Barra, and very scarce in North Uist.

The other British hare, the brown hare, a bigger animal with longer ears and black on the top of its tail, seems to have come to Harris and Lewis at the same time but soon died out. This is not surprising really, since the brown hare is a creature of the corn fields and open woodland.

Brownish-grey in summer with longish ears, tipped with black, and a long loping stride, the blue hare produces two or three litters a year of two to four leverets from March until August. These are raised separately in "forms", shallow, grass-lined depressions, or short peat burrows.

During the autumn, the summer coat is replaced by a denser, warmer coat of white which, in the snow covered highlands, must give valuable protection against fox and eagle. But here, in the Western Isles, where snow is infrequent and short-lived, this change of colour must only be a disadvantage and may, possibly, have contributed to the blue hare's decrease in numbers.

All the winter hares of which I have been told have had a mottled coat and it may be that a sub-species, similar to the Irish hare, is evolving, which remains brown and which will therefore adapt itself eventually to our environment.

The hare is the main food of the golden eagle but here it has few enemies other than the common enemy of all wild creatures, man. It is a harmless herbivore, living mainly on heather and cotton grass in summer, and gorse, juniper and soft rush in winter according to research carried out by a former colleague of mine, Raymond Hewson, in 1962. Only in excessive numbers may their presence be resented by foresters for the wanton damage they do to young trees, a situation unlikely to arise in these islands.

The Hatter shook his head mournfully. "Not I!" he replied. "We quarrelled last March — just before he went mad, you know..." (pointing with his teaspoon at the March Hare).

During the breeding season, hares gather in groups and sit around motionless then suddenly disperse with a great burst of activity, hence, presumably, the reputation for madness which the Mad Hatter imputed at Alice's teaparty in Wonderland. And Brer Rabbit's origin was, it seems, a West African hare, whose flesh implanted cowardice in the eater and whose name came to western ears through the folklore of the American negroes.

A Customs Seal

A grey seal pup attracted a good deal of attention before being found dead on Cuddy Point. On at least two occasions, it had been stranded on adjacent beaches and been carefully returned to the water by passing pedestrians. A post mortem examination revealed that it was only 3½ feet long, weighed 31 lbs, was inordinately thin and had probably starved to death.

British grey seals breed normally in autumn, but occasionally a late pup is born in February, as occurs in the Baltic population. This little chap must have been born between these dates and had either lost or been abandoned by its mother.

There are two species of seals commonly found in the Western Isles, the large grey seal, usually 6 to 8 feet in length, and the smaller common seal which rarely exceeds 6 feet. Their size cannot easily be assessed when submerged, when the shape of the head is the best guide. The grey seal has a patrician profile with a long pointed nose while the common resembles a spaniel with blunt dog-like face. Those in Stornoway Harbour, which gave the tourist and Lewisman alike so much pleasure are, of course, grey seals.

There are eleven grey seal breeding stations in the Western Isles, the largest of which, North Rona, contains about one seventh of the world population and where some 2,500 pups are born annually. It is an eerie experience to spend a middle watch alone at anchor off North Rona, invisible seals soughing and grunting all around, their weird conversation echoing from the great cliffs.

The voice of the common seal is, on the other hand, seldom heard. This species is almost entirely confined to the Southern Isles, frequenting, in the main, the Sounds of Harris and Barra. Unlike the grey seal, which will climb as far from the sea as possible before calving and whose young are not at home in the sea for some time, the common seal calves on sea-girt rock or sandbank and takes its young into the sea almost at once.

Both species were once wastefully and cruelly exploited for their oil and skins in these islands to the point of extinction, but the advent of paraffin and "wellies" saved the common seal, and the law, the grey seal.

Two other species have occasionally turned up in the Western Isles; the walrus, which needs, surely, no introduction and the harp or Greenland seal, which is about the size of the grey seal but with a black head and blackish markings along its back.

Miscellany

The Enchanted Islands

The Shiant Islands lie only four miles from the coast of Lewis, 18 miles from Tarbert and 25 miles from Stornoway and yet are probably the least known of all the Western Isles. They were last inhabited in 1879 by a shepherd and his wife and family of three girls and a boy who would have lived in a house on a site presently occupied by one reconstructed by Sir Compton Mackenzie. This house is on the southernmost of the three islands comprising the group, Eilean an Tighe, which is joined to Eilean Garbh by a narrow boulder beach covered at exceptional spring tides. To the east-ward lies Eilean Mhuire.

A landing is difficult at the best of times but one has a choice, depending on the direction of the prevailing swell, of either side of the isthmus joining the two main islands and the wet feet and effort involved are well worth while.

The name "Shiant" may be derived from early religious occupation but it is easy to believe, once ashore for a while, that it has more magical associations. Although so close to Lewis, the Shiants are more akin geologically to Skye, being composed of igneous rock called basalt, and are the most northerly outlier of a range of this rock stretching south to the Giant's Causeway in Antrim. On Eilean Garbh the enormous pillars of basalt are, according to Harvie-Brown and others, 499 feet high and 27 times higher than the comparable, better known pillars in Staffin. Sailing under these awe-inspiring, fluted columns on a still summer's day is a memorable experience.

Equally unforgettable is the myriad bird population of all three islands. A gunshot or blast on the siren while lying in the angle formed by the islands will darken the sky with swarms of puffins from the grassy slopes of Eilean Mhuire, razorbills from the huge scree on Eilean Garbh and guillemots from the cliff ledges. There are immense colonies of all these species (e.g. 70,000 pairs of puffins, 3,000 pairs of razorbills and an equal number of guillemots are estimated to breed on the Shiants) together with innumerable gulls, kittiwakes, shags, fulmars and some eider.

One of the last eyries of the white-tailed eagle or erne was to be found in 1868 high on the east side of Eilean Garbh in a site since occupied by golden eagle until recent times. Sir Compton Mackenzie, who purchased the islands from Lord Leverhume and sold them in 1936 to the present owner, Nigel Nicolson, held them in great affection. Shortly before his death he wrote to me asking about certain plants which had thrived when he lived there. I was unable to identify them but I was astonished at the variety of plant life.

Eilean Mhuire seems to have been extensively cultivated judging by the corrugations of former lazy beds and still possesses a green sward rich in orchis, vetch, sorrel, buttercup, tormentil and many others.

Eilean an Tighe is rougher and wetter but has, neverthe-less, a surprisingly varied vegetation, including wild rose, aspen, willow, heather and honeysuckle. Lacking a head for heights I have not explored Eilean Garbh beyond the scree, but was impressed by the colourful clumps of red campion and roseroot in startling contrast with the dark satanic cliffs.

A Day in the Peats

"Sweet are the uses of adversity . . . and this our life . . . finds tongues in trees, books in the running brooks, sermons in stones, and good in everything".

So said Shakespeare. But he who is up to his elbows and knees in viscous, adhesive peat has less romantic notions of the tree roots and stones which get in his way and the rivulets of tawny water in his boots. He is more likely to find good only in a hot bath at the end of it. Peat they say, is nine-tenths water, about 6,000 years old and of two main types.

No-one will argue about the water, least of all he who throws, and the only two types of peats he recognises are large thick and small thin ones and he prefers the latter. He who wields the "tairisgear" on the other hand, sees from his loftier, more detached, viewpoint the hydricity of peat as irrelevant and is concerned only with the two kinds, sedge and black peat, and the whereabouts of his companion's right toe. Neither may be interested in the fact that when they have finished the bank they will have cut through two or three centuries of history — but it is a thought!

I have read somewhere that, on average, peat grows at the rate of about one foot every hundred years but it must be remembered that the lower layers have been flattened and compressed by later deposits and much water. The Callanish Stones, said to have been erected some 4,000 years ago, were almost covered by peat when Sir James Matheson had the peat removed. It seems that when peat began to be laid down the climate was even colder and wetter than it is now!

The high rainfall, low evaporation and a general coldness prevented normal bacterial activity in the waterlogged soil but not enough to prevent growth of vegetation. Lack of lime and other ameliorating conditions produced an acid, airless complex of withered heather, grasses, sedge and moss which we call peat. Thus one finds hard, brittle black peat above rock which burns like coal, and soft fibrous brown slow-burning peat above. Where the decomposition of the latter is incomplete, uncut fibres clog the blade, ruin the temper and jar the gastrocnemius.

The passing stranger may be forgiven for asking "What good thing can come out of the primeval amorphous stuff?" and be converted beyond doubt when shown a well made peat fire and enabled to sniff the turbinaceous blue smoke on the still night air.

Apart from the endless chatter which emanates from an exclusively female team, there is much to hear and much to watch. A day in the peats may be the only occasion in the year on which some folk will have the opportunity to hear the beautiful and ephemeral spring call of the golden plover, the mewing of a buzzard, the thin whistle of sandpipers or the trilling of dunlin. One is on a level with the moorland itself and can appreciate the beauty of the golden tormentil, the nascent emerald rosettes of the butterwort and even the tiny but intensely scarlet heads of the lichen, cladonia.

Perhaps adversity has its uses after all!

Golden eagle

Lady Lever Park

Let us go for a walk in Lady Lever Park. A little stream runs through it and our path meanders up one side and then the other. Here swallows and housemartins hawk flies but at this time of year we might be lucky enough to see goldfinches feeding on the thistle seedheads, redpolls in the alders or a wandering waterhen skulking in the long grass. Blue tits nest in a hole in a tree on our left and a pair of bullfinches were once seen by the late Professor Meiklejohn in the hedge opposite.

As we cross a bridge, two or three sombre evergreen holm oaks stand out among the leafless beeches and sycamores and, further along, a solitary walnut tree hangs its often fruitless branches over the path. If we pause under the next bridge and look carefully at the trees now closing in on us on all sides, we may glimpse a treecreeper spiralling his acrobatic way up a trunk or branch in search of insects in the crevices of the bark or among the lichen or hear goldcrest as they flit busily about the treetops above. The needle-sharp piping of these, the smallest of our birds, is almost inaudible and the older one gets, the less audible it seems to be.

A water-mill once occupied the opposite bank. The outlines of its foundations can still be discerned and the bed of the mill-lade traced along the high bank, in a hole in which a great tit sometimes nests. A grove of cypress appears ahead of us in a clearing; Lawson cypress, named after John Lawson who explored North Carolina in 1800 and, presumably, found this elegant tree growing there whence, since 1854, it has been introduced into the old world.

Here one may watch spotted flycatchers in summer. These are the last of the summer visitors to arrive, any time after the 15th May, and their upright stance and quite unique habit of brief flights from a favourite perch after passing flies puts their identity beyond doubt.

As the glen narrows, great conifers throw a perennial shadow across our path, now almost overgrown with that euphoniously named plant Luzula sylvatica or woodrush, but not so deeply that the dapper grey wagtail, with his bright yellow breast, escapes notice as he flashes upstream. Once the dipper could also be seen here but tar and sewage have effectively killed the small fish he lived on.

Is it too much to hope that such pollution will soon cease and this delightful glen enjoy the protection from development intended by its founder?

The holm oak and the walnut trees already mentioned are, as far as can be ascertained, the only ones of their kind in the Western Isles and surely deserve especial protection.

Those of you who live in Stornoway will probably have guessed that we have been walking up the Bayhead Burn and Willowglen.

The Vanishing Peregrine

It is possible that one of our most spectacular and rarest birds is on the way out.

Like the white-tailed eagle, osprey, kite and others, the peregrine falcon may soon disappear from the Scottish Highlands and Islands as a result of man's insatiable greed. The 'seabhag' has always been in demand for falconry for no other falcon possesses its speed and dashing flight in the pursuit of prey. The tiercel or male bird is slightly smaller than the eighteen inch female or falcon.

It is our largest native falcon and is easily distinguished by its dark slate-blue plumage and pointed, sweptback wings. At close quarters the dark moustache-like markings are conspicuous. It preys mainly on pigeons but can kill a bird as large as a great black-backed gull, which should be enough to endear it to any islander. Towering high above its prey the peregrine half-closes its wings and stoops at tremendous speed striking the unfortunate creature with outstretched talons and usually killing it instantly.

Its fondness for pigeons drastically reduced the English population for the pigeons had fed on grain dressed with chlorinated hydrocarbons, now illegal, and the build-up of poison in the falcon eventually caused its death, or, at least, infertility. In December 1971, a tiercel was found dead in Ness and autopsy confirmed that its death was due to just such causes.

Many readers will have read in the national press of the theft of eggs and young of this species in the Highlands and Islands by organised gangs. Although once common, the peregrine is now a very rare bird in these islands and such despicable racketeers may not consider the journey worthwhile. Nevertheless, where a species is so close to extinction in a discrete area like this every single bird is important, and will be vulnerable in the face of general apathy. One islander when asked in connection with the present harrassment of our golden eagles if he did not care that his children might never see an eagle replied that he couldn't care less. It is this irresponsible attitude to our wild life that is worrying.

Peregrine falcon

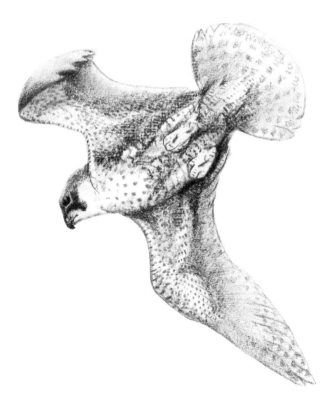

It is an offence under the Protection of Birds Act 1967, to take the eggs or young of a specially protected species like the peregrine which incurs a heavy penalty and it is also an offence even to disturb a breeding peregrine on the nest except under licence.

The Quiet Invasion

In 1930, they were confined to Asia. Ten years later they had invaded Europe as far as Austria and in another decade had reached the shores of the North Sea and Scandinavia.

On 15th June, 1960, I saw the first one to be seen in the west of Scotland perched on a tree in the Castle Grounds. An eminent ornithologist who visited Lewis a day or two later reported another in Coulregrein but decently conceded the honour of seeing the most westerly collared dove in Europe to me! According to Robert Hudson, who has written a comprehensive account of this odyssey, the rapidity of the collared doves' spread across the entire continent is almost without precedent.

This slim grey bird with a black half-collar and a dove's innocent expression, scarcely seems robust enough for such wanderings. Nevertheless, it is a fact that, driven by some hidden vital compulsion, successive generations have pushed 3,000 miles into the unknown to the very Atlantic itself. The same impulse which has driven the doves westward over the North Sea to unseen Britain is still driving them westward over the Atlantic.

Iceland has recently been colonised and it is only a matter of time before they find the New World, many doubtless perishing in the attempt. Since they are easily fed with grain, assisted passages in ships may enable them to accomplish the journey more safely.

Although they are said to produce up to five broods a year, a potent factor in their expansion, few nests have been found in the Western Isles and it was two years before they were first proved to breed in Lewis. On 7th October, 1962, I received a peremptory summons from the late Colin Scott Mackenzie, Procurator Fiscal, and hastened to his office in Lewis Street in some trepidation. All he did on my arrival, however, was to ask what kind of bird was breeding in a slight nest in a sycamore where St. Columba's Manse now stands, a few yards from his window. The two squabs indicated were the first collared doves to have their births registered in the Western Isles.

By 1966, thirty doves could be counted at Goathill Farm and yet only one other nest was found in a cypress beside the Castle. One pair later adopted the strange environment of the gantry at the Shell Oil Depot and brought up young within feet of staff replenishing the road tankers. By this time, (1969), North Uist had been colonised and nests were found under the eaves of the schoolhouse at Sollas and on a waste-pipe outside a bathroom in Newton House Hotel.

South Uist also has its colony of a score or so but so far during my brief visits to Barra I have not encountered any on the island.

The cuckoo-like call of the collared dove sometimes deceives the uninitiated and I used to be told of cuckoos calling three times instead of twice. However, once heard, the distinctive call cannot be confused with that of any other bird, comprising three calls, with the emphasis on the middle one and a falling cadence and without the difference of pitch which characterises the cuckoo's call. But it can be just as annoying as the cuckoo at an unreasonably early hour in the morning. So much so in fact that I am at a loss as to why it came to be called a "quiet invasion".

Biblical Plants

"And God said, "Behold, I have given you every herb bearing seed, which is upon the face of all the earth and every tree, — And the Lord God planted a garden, eastward in Eden".

The most famous, or infamous, fruit in this garden was, of course, that of the tree of knowledge, popularly believed to be an apple but nowhere in Genesis referred to as such. It is, in fact, generally considered that where the apple is referred to, in for example Proverbs 25, verse 11, "A word fitly spoken is like apples of gold in pictures of silver", it is the apricot that is meant.

There is no doubt that of the sixty odd other plants mentioned in the Authorised Version, the vine is the commonest.

Noah first planted a vineyard and he lost no time in falling under its influence. Naboth found his inheritance of a vineyard an embarrassment. Jesus used the symbol of the many-branched vine tellingly in some of his parables and teaching.

As in the case of birds and animals, I find it interesting to realise that many of the plants in the Bible are those known to us. Isaiah mentions cedars, cypress, oak and ash, all of which are found in Stornoway woods, though there are only two or three cedars and holm oaks.

It seems that the Victorian painter, Alma-Tadema, used the great reed-mace or false bulrush in his well known picture of Moses as an infant, since when it has usurped the name of bulrush from the true plant, of which the little ark was made and which grows, as far as I know, only in Bragar in Lewis. One would like to think that the "flags" amongst which the ark was found were the same yellow irises which grace many a Hebridean roadside in summer but they were more likely a kind of sedge.

Again, the beautiful metaphor in Song of Solomon "I am the rose of Sharon and the lily of the valleys" should apparently be more correctly translated as "the asphodelic of Sharon and the iris of the valleys", but how prosaic in comparison!

Zacchaeus was a tax-gatherer and it might be inferred from his agility in climbing trees and his subsequent undertakings as to the disposal of his wealth that he was (unlike some we know) an unscrupulous one. A minor but interesting point in Luke's story is that it was not, as many believe, a familiar sycamore he climbed but a species of fig-tree which, on account of its spreading habit and grateful shade was often planted by the Palestinian roadside.

The burning bush whence God recalled Moses to duty was probably one of the acacias, a useful member of the same family as the pea. It is said that its incorruptible wood was used by the Egyptians to make coffins for their kings and by the Jews for the Ark of the Covenant.

Biblical Birds

A photograph of the first lamb of 1976 and the Communion Season in Stornoway turned my mind to the frequent references to the earth's living creatures in the Authorised Version of the Bible.

Thanks to the industry of the compilers of Cruden's Concordance, it is possible to estimate that about 65 plants, 56 animals including insects and 26 birds are mentioned in the Old and New Testament.

Many receive specific mention and therefore stick in the mind like the sycamore climbed by Zacchaeus, the "Lamb" of God and the dove released by Noah in his quest for dry land. And it is, in particular, the birds I wish to discuss today.

Consider the beautiful reference to the maternal instinct of the hen in Psalm 17, "hide me under the shadow of thy wings" or Jesus' rebuke to Jerusalem ending with the imperishable "as a hen gathereth her chickens under her wings". How splendid the Psalmist's picture of the wrath of God when he "did fly upon the wings of the wind" or his prayer for "wings like a dove" to "take the wings of the morning" and, like Isaiah, "mount up with wings as eagles".

Similar poetic references occur in Solomon's Song and one which particularly appeals to me is that harbinger of spring "the voice of the turtle (which) is heard in our land". For it is often in May that the occasional turtle dove visits these islands and, of course, everybody is familiar now with the tri-syllabic call of the collared dove.

Jesus uses a bird metaphor very effectively when he illustrates the omniscience of the Father by reference to the humble sparrow "Are not two sparrows sold for a farthing? and one of them shall not fall on the ground without your Father". Is not the message brought home to us by the knowledge that the house sparrow to which

He referred are the same and as numerous as those we know?

In the same way, other birds like the eagle, hoopoe, cormorant and raven are also of the same species, while many which passed through Palestine on migration to or from Africa also pass through the Western Isles but using a different, more westerly route across the Straits of Gibralter or the Malta/Italy bridge. Examples of the latter are osprey, quail, cuckoo and the swallow.

The longest catalogue of birds in the bible is, of course, in the list in Deuteronomy and Leviticus of creatures deemed to be unclean by the orthodox Jew, whereby he was forbidden the pleasure of eating vultures, ospreys and 16 other species, not to mention bats and beetles.

In some instances, the remarkable detail contained in the Authorised Version can mislead.

In Psalm 102 David likens his distress so evocatively to a "pelican in the wilderness", in which place such a bird would be in real trouble for its natural habitat is by water. The New English Bible however, translates the original word as "desert owl".

Again, in the Authorised Version, God convinces Job of his ignorance by asking him if he can, among other feats, give the peacock its "goodly wings" or the ostrich its wings and feathers, but the New English Bible which ought to be a more authentic translation, refers only to the ostrich. This is reasonable for the peacock is a native of India, although we are told that Solomon imported peacocks from Ophir. Nevertheless, it is fascinating to read in both versions an accurate account of the peculiar habit of the ostrich "which leaveth her eggs in the earth, and warmeth them in the dust".

Jeremiah compares the ignorance of his contemporaries with the wisdom of the stork, crane, dove and swallow, which know when to migrate for the good of the species. Neither we nor the birds seem to have changed much.

Biblical Animals

"Agus mar chaora bhios balbh an làthair a luchd-iomart, mar sin cha'n fhosgail e a bheul. And as a sheep before her shearers is dumb, so he openeth not his mouth".

That these prophetic words of Isaiah were taken from life will be obvious to anyone who has attended a fank in summer. The mute acquiescence of the victim is in sharp contrast to the babble outside the fank.

There are probably more references to sheep and lambs in the Bible than to any other single creature and the historicity of this phenomenon is beyond the scope of this article; it is sufficient to point to the effectiveness of the metaphorical references to the Paschal lamb, the symbol of innocence, vicarious suffering, sacrifice and redemption, leading to John the Baptist's naming of Christ as the Lamb of God and to the shepherd and the sheep symbolism with which we are all familiar.

The first of the remaining fifty odd animals referred to in the Bible is the whale: "And God created great whales". In my ignorance, I thought that "behemoth", "leviathan" referred to the whale but I see now that the hippopotamus and crocodile respectively are meant.

Talking of whales, Jonah is always associated with a whale, but the Authorised Version and the New English Bible say he was in the belly of "a great fish" which is not quite the same thing. Incidentally, there is a theory that the story is an allegory, Jonah representing Israel overwhelmed by the great fish of Babylon before repentance.

The Israelites had other ways, however, of getting round their troubles and the poor goat was the means: the "scapegoat" which, after a symbolic ceremony, was pushed over a cliff, taking the nation's sins with it.

Other animals which must excite our sympathy were the donkey and the pig. The former was used everywhere as a long-suffering beast of burden, but he had his triumph as described by G K Chesterton in his poem ending with the lines, "For I also had my hour; one fierce hour and sweet. There was a shout about my ears and palms before my feet!"

The pig is represented as the lowest to which man can stoop, as in the case of the Prodigal Son, who found himself in his extremity, feeding swine. They were also a convenient beast to throw pearls before and transfer devils into.

As I mentioned before, Solomon was responsible for the importation of some of the biblical creatures into Palestine as has been gracefully described by John Masefield in "Cargoes".

"Quinquireme of Nineveh from distant Ophir, rowing home to haven in sunny Palestine, with a cargo of ivory, and apes and peacocks, sandalwood, cedarwood, and sweet white wine".

Disappearing Birds

I have noted the apparent disappearance of the dipper from the Bayhead Burn in Stornoway.

The dipper is a harmless and interesting creature. It has been persecuted for feeding on salmon and sea trout eggs, but I am of the opinion that it cleanses the stream by eating the infertile and free-floating eggs, the fertile eggs being well protected below inches of gravel. It is one of the earliest birds to nest and this may account for the decrease.

The peregrine falcon is so rare in the Western Isles now as to be in danger of extinction. Apart from illegal robbing of eyries for eggs or young for falconry, our peregrines suffer from the fact that they prey to a large extent on sea birds which have absorbed toxic chemicals from plankton and small fish poisoned by effluent from American industries carried by the Gulf Stream and the Atlantic Drift. One peregrine found dying in Ness some years ago was found to have built up a lethal quantity of such substances in its body.

Many elderly people have brought my attention to the scarcity of smaller birds nowadays on our moors compared to the numbers seen in their youth. In my opinion, this is almost entirely due to the havoc wrought by the hooded crow and great black-backed gull which can now be seen all over these islands in appalling profusion. No nest or young bird is safe from their insatiable maws.

In the last twenty years or so, the greylag goose has decreased alarmingly as a breeding species. Man is the guilty party in this instance by indiscriminate shooting, thoughtless burning of heather on breeding islands and stealing eggs for setting under domestic hens. So has the greylag been exterminated in many areas.

Every person who takes an egg or young bird of the species I have mentioned, is bringing their disappearance from our islands one step nearer.

The Great Auk

Icelandic sagas tell of a great multitude of auks on Skerries east of Greenland found by 12th century Norse voyagers from Iceland to the New World and furnish us with the first evidence of their existence. It is likely that, in prehistoric times, this species was abundant in the palearctic region from Newfoundland to Northern Europe but was driven from the American continent by the Red Indian who hunted it for food. Settling on remote islands beyond the reach of his canoes, it was safe for a time until men began to venture into the Arctic and gain access, once again, to their breeding areas. Any hunted species is safe from extinction until exploited during breeding, when advantage is taken of its comparative helplessness or devotion to its young.

Standing 32 inches high, these huge flightless relations of the razorbill, were at the mercy of man on land and were driven on board ships over planks in their hundreds to feed crews during the long sea voyages into the New World which began in the 16th century.

Funk Island off Newfoundland, the Magdalen Islands in the Gulf of St. Lawrence, the Icelandic Westmann Islands, St. Kilda and Papa Westray were the main breeding grounds where the great auk shambled ashore in spring to lay a single egg.* This egg was about 5 inches long and 3 inches diameter at its widest part for, like those of most auks it was pyriform, or conical, in shape to prevent it rolling off the nesting ledge and white or blue-green in colour, streaked, blotched or spotted with dark brown.

A very efficient swimmer, the great auk was not properly adapted for life on land and it is supposed that the young birds left the nest "not much more than a fortnight after hatching".

The first authentic description of the great auk was given by the Lord Register, Sir George MacKenzie of Tarbat in 1682 who tells that "on St. Kilda there be many sorts of fowls; some of them of strange shapes among which there is one they call the gare fowl, which is bigger than any goose, and hatch eggs as big almost as those of the ostrich".

In 1697, Martin Martin provides what sounds like an eye-witness description of the bird, "Gairfow, being the stateliest as well as the largest sort, and above the size of a solan goose, of a black colour, red about the eyes, a large white spot under each, a long broad bill; it stands stately, its whole body erected, its wings short, flies not at all; lays its eggs upon the bare rock, which, if taken away, she lays no more for that year".

Human greed must have reduced their numbers so drastically that when five St. Kildans catching birds on Stac an Armin in 1840, came across a great auk, it was so strange to them that they thought it was a witch and in their superstitious terror stoned the poor creature to death. So died the last great auk in Scotland.

For years its passing was not known, and it was sought high and low by naturalists. The devoted interest of those ornithologists only served to show that ornithology came not quite in time to save the auk, and that ignorance and greed are sometimes more powerful than knowledge and truth.

* "Sea Birds" Fisher and Lockley Collins 1954

Birds in Folklore

In the "Legend of the Kingfisher", Longfellow recounts how Noah sent forth a kingfisher after the first dove. Now the kingfisher was then an ordinary grey bird and it was bored with life on the Ark. It didn't bother looking for land but flew higher and higher until the sky stained its back blue and the sun burned its breast red. In fact, it flew so high that it couldn't find the Ark again and to this day is still flying up and down water looking for it.

But the dove returned the second time and "in her mouth was an olive leaf", since when this gentle and harmless bird has become the emblem of peace and a symbol of the Holy Ghost. The soft susurrant call of turtle dove or pigeon has become the sound of mourning since Hezekiah, sick unto death, "did mourn as a dove".

The embodiment of innocence and purity, the dove was so prized as a prime sacrifice that the inordinate Temple traffic in them led to its cleansing at the hands of Jesus.

The gentleness of the robin is, however, more legendary than factual. It was the contemporary ubiquity of the likeness of this species on Christmas cards and elsewhere that prompted these thoughts. Formerly drab like the kingfisher, the breast of this belligerent little creature became, it is said, drenched in blood as it tried to remove Christ's crown of thorns. Another legend has it that the unique crossed mandibles of the crossbill, so effective in removing seed from tough fir cones, really became distorted when the bird wrestled with the nails on the Cross.

The duck also, but who knows what species, invoked divine favour when it was supposed to have concealed Jesus under straw when pursued and then along came the accursed hen which inquisitively scratched away the straw and exposed Him to His enemies.

So also is the lapwing hated in certain parts of Scotland for having betrayed the Covenanters in the hills with its restless cries.

Apart, perhaps, from the redshank, the most "alarming" bird is the oystercatcher, whose bidding "bi glic, bi glic" (be wise, be wise) befits a bird under the protection of the patron saint of birds, St. Bride, and therefore called by some "gille brìde".

In Eriskay, I believe, the familiar skylark is associated with an even more exalted person where it is known as "uiseag Mhuire" or Mary's lark.

Certain birds are regarded with superstition which tends to die hard in a seafaring community. Time was when a fisherman would turn back on meeting a red-haired woman or any member of the crow family; for all I know they may still feel inclined to do so on such encounters.

Oystercatchers

An implausible but accepted explanation at one time for the disappearance in autumn of the wheatear, cuckoo and corncrake was that they disappeared underground with the fairies and thereby acquired a certain awesomeness, becoming known as "eòin shìthe" and giving rise to the saying "chunnaic mi'n clacharan air cloich lium". So wait until your first wheatear takes to the wing before spotting him!

It is just as well that we in the Western Isles, with our wealth of birds of ill omen are spared the magpie.

The preponderance of evil related to the number of magpies seen at one time, especially before breakfast, is appalling. the Braham Seer is recorded as saying:

> "Chunnaic mi Pioghaid is dh'éirich leam
> Chunnaic mi dhà's gum b'iarguin iad
> Chunnaic mi trì a's b'aihearach mi
> Ach ceithir ri m'linn cha'n iarainn iad.

> I saw a magpie, to me then luck did die
> I once saw two and they troubled me
> Great joy was on me when once I saw three
> But four forever let me not see".

There are also the well known current rhymes about magpies: "One is a birth, two sorrow, three a wedding and four a death", and "One for sorrow, two for joy, three for a girl and four for a boy".

I leave it to my readers to apportion the amount of evil in each saying.

Dr J W Campbell

I have been privileged to read some of the notes left by the late Dr. James W. Campbell.

His family had Newton House, North Uist, in the 1930's and he was a regular visitor to these islands during his lifetime. He studied the bird-life and ornithological literature of the Western Isles with much care and sympathy and it had been his intention to publish these notes in a book which would bring together all the contemporary knowledge of the numbers and distribution of our birds in much the same way as Harvie-Brown had done in 1888.

Dr Campbell's death in 1970 prevented publication of his book but his notes provide sufficient material for an important contribution to British ornithological literature in which he will live in the memory of those of us who held him in affection and in the regard of those who have the welfare of our wildlife at heart.

Dr Campbell's painstaking research into the writings and reports of naturalists, gamekeepers and shooting tenants since attention was first paid to the natural history of the Outer Hebrides reveals many interesting features.

He quotes, for example, a tradition in Berneray, Harris, that the longtailed duck "is still known as McCandlay-eun (McCandlay's bird), which arose, as reported by Alexander Carmichael to Harvie-Brown, from a fancied resemblance in its voice to the name McCandlay — a family name in Berneray — where it is considered by the natives as a harbinger or herald of winter".

There are no McCandlay's left on Berneray according to the Electoral Roll but it would be interesting to know if this beautiful and endearing duck is still associated with them.

Dr Campbell reminds us, in his notes on the sanderling, one of the smallest of our waders, whose conspicuously white winter plumage and busy little black legs distinguish it on our winter beaches, that the attractive bungalow on Barra's Tràigh Mhór was called "Sanderling Cottage" by its first owner, the Duchess of Bedford, whence she used to watch them on one of their favourite strands.

Records

The Guinness Book of Animal Facts and Feats (G.J. Wood, 1976) is a fascinating collection of extremes in the animal kingdom, to which my attention was drawn by an article in the "Banffshire Journal".

With my predilection for birds I noted a few examples of these extremes relating to birds which may be of general interest.

The golden eagle naturally features largely under various heads. For instance, it is one of the longest living birds, (Psalm 103:5) 104 years being recorded for one individual. Its eyesight is legendary, being capable, it is said, of detecting a one inch grasshopper at 300 yards! The wingspan of a golden eagle at 9ft. 4 ins. is only 2ft. shorter than that of the world's greatest, that of the wandering albatross.

This magnificent bird, familiar to mariners, ancient and modern, from these islands, may soar for six hours without a wingbeat while the humming bird needs 90 beats a second to keep going. This species is the smallest in the world at 2¼ ins. and yet it uses 155,000 calories of energy a day compared with man's 3,500. Our own smallest bird, the goldcrest, for the sake of comparison, is more than an inch longer at 3½ ins.

One of the heaviest birds of prey mentioned in the book was the white-tailed eagle which was shot at Stornoway in the 19th century and weighed 16½ lbs. There is an amusing reference to the great sulphur crested cockatoo which was said to have been 120 years old when he died in Sydney in 1916. Formerly in the possession of a skipper of a sailing ship, "Cocky Bennet" was almost featherless for the last 25 years of his life and was often heard to scream "One more ****** feather and I'll be able to fly".

There are some 10,000 million red-billed queleas in the world, making it the most abundant species. There were 5 to 9 thousand million passenger pigeons in America until the white man arrived and slaughtered the lot; which just goes to show how beastly we can be when we try.

No one living near isolated trees in the Western Isles will be surprised to learn that there are about 2,000 million starlings in the world. They come second to blackbirds as the most abundant garden species in this country, followed by the house sparrow, blue tit, robin, greenfinch, hedge sparrow, great tit, song thrush and chaffinch. The most abundant British seabird is the fulmar petrel at 100,000 pairs and yet peope still alive can remember when they first came to the U.K. from St. Kilda.

The Arctic tern holds the record for travelling, performing a 24,000 mile journey each year between the Poles, while the sooty tern is the most aerial bird, spending the first 3 or 4 years without settling on land or water. And our own common swift is remarkable for its ability to remain constantly on the wing for nine months of the year.

Speed, of course, must be mentioned. I was under the impression that the delightful and elusive American Roadrunner of TV cartoon fame was a figment of someone's imagination, but this species does in fact hold the world land speed record for birds at 26 mph. On the other hand, the fastest flying bird is the spine-tailed swift which has clocked 106 mph. I thought the peregrine falcon held the record for diving and level flight but at 82 and 60 mph respectively it is comparatively slow: one of the illusions shattered by this extremely readable and interesting book.

A catalogue of Birds

Check Lists relating to different areas of the United Kingdom and discrete parts of the world have been published from time to time and found to be of great value to students and visitors alike. The only list in existence for these islands as a whole was published in 1888 by J.A. Harvie-Brown and is now obsolete. He noted some 155 species whereas the present total numbers 265. Some, like the white-tailed eagle and great auk, are now extinct; others, like the fulmar petrel, blue and great tit, and collared dove are now commonplace.

A symposium was held in Edinburgh in 1978 under the auspices of the Nature Conservancy Council and the Royal Society of Edinburgh in which the whole field of natural history of the Western Isles was described and discussed by experts in each discipline. The list of subjects was formidable and included esoteric studies such as the macrofauna of the inter-tidal sand, the polychaetous annelids and a new concept of glaciation in the Outer Hebrides to some of more general interest like the grey seal problem and a review of our fish and shellfish resources.

Perhaps the most important result of the Symposium has been the collation of all the thirty-one papers in a book similar to that already produced for the Orkney Islands, in which the vast and varied research and observations of a great many trained scientists, heretofore tucked away in University files or published with limited circulation, will be available for all to read.

It is a very exciting prospect and shows that these islands are at last receiving the attention they so richly deserve. The Check List I have referred to reflects this attention for it was necessary to include the work of such institutions as Leicester University, the Royal Air Force and the Schools Hebridean Society, eminent ornithologists such as Dr J W Campbell and publications of the calibre of the *"Scottish Naturalist"* and *"Scottish Birds"*.

The variety of exotic species appearing in the current List leaves one gasping. Personal acquaintance with snowy owls, flamingoes and spoonbills might have rendered one blasé in this connection but, fortunately, I could still find it possible to gasp as I read of, say a white-throated sparrow on the Flannans in 1909, of a red-spotted bluethroat on the Monachs in 1888 and an eyebrowed thrush on North Rona in 1964. Such rarities are undoubtedly more easily recognised on these relatively small islands but it is equally beyond doubt that they have occurred in the Long Island but have not been seen by the few people able to identify them, from maybe only a brief glimpse. Too often I receive belated reports of an unusual bird when it has flown beyond our ken and which might have proved to be a rare or even an unprecedented visitor to the Western Isles.

Oiled Birds

A pamphlet *"Oiled Birds — What to do"* published by the RSPB states that the one thing which should NOT be used in the treatment of oiled birds is detergent, for the very same reason given by me elsewhere — that it removes the natural oil in the plumage along with the unwanted oil.

The "Torrey Canyon" disaster in March 1967 emphasised the need for urgent contingency planning at local, national and international levels. Official schemes have now been prepared and the Western Isles Islands Council have the necessary knowledge and material to deal with limited pollution of our coastal waters. No one who has visited any of our seabird cliffs in the breeding season will underestimate the deadly effect of an oil spillage near, say, the Shiant Islands or Barra Head.

A walk along any of the beaches at any time of year will usually throw up a dead or dying bird, clarted with filthy oil which it has picked up off-shore in an oil-slick deposited by a passing ship while pumping bilges or cleaning tanks.

Apart from losing its buoyancy and unable, therefore, to feed, a bird so affected will inevitably swallow oil in an attempt to clean its feathers. Such birds as guillemots, divers, grebes, mergansers, sea ducks and waders have little chance of survival, even if lightly oiled, and should be humanely killed.

Diving ducks, geese, swans and cormorants have a better chance.

If however, you wish to clean an oiled bird the following treatment is suggested.

1 All oiled birds will be in a state of shock and should not be frightened (e.g. by being chased unnecessarily) and should be handled with great care.

2 Wrap the bird in an absorbent cloth except for its head and feet so that it cannot preen.

3 Place it in a suitable container and sprinkle the oiled plumage with Fuller's Earth.

4 If the oil does not fall away after a night's rest it must be softened with edible oil (e.g. margarine) and again dusted with Fuller's Earth until clean.

5 Keep the bird at room temperature until it has recovered its strength and is taking appropriate food: "Complan", Scott's Emulsion or cod liver oil is recommended at first to get rid of ingested oil.

6 Follow the advice given elsewhere in connection with convalescence and release.

If the bird cannot be identified or is ringed on the leg, I shall be glad to hear about it.

The RSPB has organised a Beached Birds Survey whereby observers record details from all round the coast which helps to assess the occurrence of oil pollution and its effects on sea-bird populations. Anyone finding evidence of oil pollution should immediately contact the Oil Pollution Officer of the Western Isles Islands Council.

A Murmuration of Starlings

The starling is considered by ornithologists to be one of the most successful birds alive today. It is found in every continent except South America and would be unknown in North America too had not one hundred been introduced into New York in 1890, which so multiplied and spread that they are now as numerous as the human population. So many native birds suffered from this invasion that the United States were forced to initiate legislation to prevent further introductions of alien species. Together with the rock dove and house sparrow, also an introduced species, the starling is the most important bird of North American cities. It has, in fact, been referred to as the "wide boy" of the bird world and no-one who has seen the swaggering gait of this jaunty little bird can doubt the aptness of the metaphor.

The starling is reckoned to be the friend of the farmer but the enemy of the fruit grower for it not only consumes vast numbers of harmful insects but also does great damage in the orchard in autumn. Man, indeed, though not essential to its existence, has created an environment which the starling exploits to its advantage.

There are said to be about seven million starlings in the United Kingdom and, of all our birds, it is the most evenly distributed, few places being without their quota of starlings. And yet, one hundred years ago, it was little known except in the Western and Northern Isles. There, a special race, called the Shetland starling, has always existed, the adults indistinguishable in the field but having darker coloured young. During the nineteenth century the species began to spread over the whole country, following man and using his city buildings as roosts instead of caves, reeds and trees. I remember an evening in Glasgow when the twittering of thousands of starlings (a murmuration) crowding the ledges in Sauchiehall Street almost drowned the roar of the traffic — before it became a pedestrian precinct. In the islands they can defoliate trees with their droppings, so closely do they crowd the branches.

Few hole-nesting birds are safe from their rapacious filibustering: the blue tit in the nest-box or the woodpecker in its chiselled cavity, both are ejected unceremoniously by the starling.

Some extraordinary nests have been recorded, but the most surprising I have come across was in the attic of a Back School building in 1968. In a depression on top of a pile of nest material measuring seven feet in length with a width and height of four feet and weighing forty-eight lbs., was a starling's nest containing three young. In the four years since the completion of the building two starlings had accumulated this astonishing quantity of leaves, feathers, scraps of paper and cloth and so on for the comfort of their offspring. Not content with stealing other birds' nests, the starling frequently steals their song, being an accomplished mimic.

In my opinion the cuckoo is about the only bird whose call it cannot reproduce but I do not despair of hearing at least a tentative imitation one day. If one hears an oystercatcher calling from a tree or the thrilling spring song of a golden plover from a rooftop in summer, a starling, with head upstretched and shaggy mane quivering, will be found to be the impersonator.

The Isle of Monks or Monach Isles

In 1549, the Reverend Donald Munro, MA, High Dean of the Isles, visited a group of five islands six miles southwest of North Uist which he called "Helsker na Caillach pertaining to the Nunnis of Comkill, gude corn land not well fyrit".

We know them as the Monach Isles or Heskeir but no one now works the good corn land nor requires fuel, for the inhabitants were evacuated in the 1940's. The monks are said to have maintained a beacon there which the Vikings doubtless found useful, for it was they who called the island the flat or ocean rock. Now the graceful tower of an eyeless lighthouse stands empty on Shillay and the houses of the eight families who entertained Seton Gordon in 1926 have been abandoned to starlings and wheatears.

These lowlying islands, 572 hectares in area and only 19 m. above sea level at the highest point are really nothing more than a drowned promontory of North Uist, comprising Shillay, Ceann Iar, Shivinish and Stockay. Dominated by shell sand, they afford rich grazing for cattle, sheep and rabbits and a glorious collection of wild flowers with the gold of buttercup, bird's foot trefoil, lady's bedstraw and heartsease and the silver of daisy and white clover.

Great flocks of geese, barnacle and whitefront, spend the winter grazing on this oasis in the wild Atlantic while the grey seals haul out to bear and suckle their pups.

In spring and autumn, a constant stream of migrant birds pass through the group. They need no lighthouse to point them on their mysterious journeys. To the redwing and geese from Iceland and Greenland they are a welcome landfall and a refuge to the Scandinavian chaffinch and brambling pushed by easterly winds to the edge of their world.

One hundred different kinds of birds have occurred on the Monachs including such rarities as the North American wader, the lesser yellowlegs, and the pretty pink Ross's gull from distant northeast Siberia. Some of the forty breeding species have had to extemporise in the matter of nesting places. Fulmar petrels have taken to the sand dunes in the absence of suitable cliffs and a pair of herons once built their nest in the rafters of an abandoned house.

The Monachs were declared a National Nature Reserve in 1966 on account of their importance to migrant birds and by virtue of their being one of the finest examples of machair and dune plant communities in the United Kingdom. Long may they remain so although it is always sad to see derelict houses and boatless harbours.

"The isles shall wait upon me, and on mine arm shall they trust".

The Islands of the Forktails

"Three men alive on Flannan Isle who thought of three men dead" — so wrote Wilfred Wilson Gibson of the tragedy which overtook the three lighthouse-keepers on the Flannan Isles soon after the light was established in 1899.

The six or seven islands and three times as many rocks, lie twenty miles west of Gallan Head, rising steeply from the 40 m. depths of the Continental Shelf to the highest point on Eilean Mor, nearly 90 m. above sea level.

The Vikings do not seem to have bothered with them since all the islands and rocks bear Gaelic names still. Indeed, although some of the larger islands have been noted since the 16th century for the fattening of sheep, and Lewismen once carried out annual raids on their puffins and other seabirds, little else of value has come out of them.

I had often gazed longingly at the squat, grey profile of the Flannans from the cliffs and hilltops of Carloway as they floated on the horizon like a squadron of aircraft carriers with attendant escorts. But access to the main island, as to the others, is difficult in anything other than a flat calm, as I found to my cost on the only occasion I tried to get ashore. I must therefore rely on more successful explorers such as J A Harvie-Brown in the yawl "Crusader" in 1881, Robert Atkinson and John Ainslie in the Bernera boat "Rhoda", whose amusing tale of their landing in 1937 is told in "Island Going" and Dr P G Hopkins in 1975 with a Nicolson Institute expedition.

Michael Robson wrote in 1957 that "In the summer evenings, wet or fine, the Flannans belong to the Leach's petrels" (Leach's forktailed petrel). These little oceanic birds, more like "sea swallows" than the terns, nest also on St. Kilda and North Rona in cairns, walls and under the turf and "fill the island tops with their purrs of joy and their searching twitters".

But it is the auks which really take over the islands in their thousands every summer; guillemots and razorbills, together with almost two thousand kittiwakes and over two thousand fulmars, teem in the cliffs on all sides while as many puffins as all the rest put together nest in the grassy plateau "like a meadow thickly enamelled with daisies" as on Dr MacCulloch's day in 1815.

It is worth noting that there is no record of gannets breeding on the Flannans until 1969, when sixteen pairs were found nesting on Roareim.

Although not so well known as the other offshore islands for their migrant birds, the Flannans are doubtless as welcome a refuge to many birds on passage and even the landlubberly collared dove was found there by Dr Hopkins in 1975. On July 13th 1908, the only collared pratincole to be recorded in the Western Isles turned up in the Flannans. It was an adult female from the sunbaked mudflats of southern Europe and must have been hard up for a mate to venture so far from home.

The short-toed lark which appeared on September 20th, 1904, must surely have been short of other faculties also to wander so far from sunny Spain. It might, however, be more charitable to assume that both were borne north willy-nilly by southerly gales like so many other Continental migrants.

Wild Flowers

There is a beautiful and interesting book in the Western Isles libraries which describes the art of preserving flowers.* Now this is something to be encouraged here, for while we do not lack flowers in quantity on the machair of the west, we are not rich in species and any means of cultivating an interest in and conservation of our flora is clearly welcome.

Mr Ian Miller, formerly of the Nicolson Institute, once recorded in a radio programme the astonishing fact that though the East Indies may possess more kinds of orchid, the Western Isles have more orchids!

We have, however, our own sub-species, the deep red Hebridean orchid, which can be found on certain Uig machairs in July. Over-picking or, worse still, removal of the entire plant, or unrestricted access by the motor car to these machairs may well bring it to the edge of extinction, as may soon happen in Orkney, from similar causes, to the rare Scottish primrose. Why not take home one or two blooms, preserve them as described in the book to which I have referred and have them as a joy forever?

While there is great pleasure to be derived from contemplation of the rich flora of the west in high summer, comprising, besides orchids, field gentian, tufted vetch, field scabious, herb robert, and many others mentioned in M.S. Campbell's *The Flora of Uig",* I think it is much more fun to seek out the more solitary flowers of cliff and moorland; to come upon a clump of brilliant red campion or roseroot tucked in a cleft of exposed sea-cliff; dark exotic cinquefoil in a marsh; royal fern, king-cup or elegant St. John's wort gracing the bank of a stream.

I remember once, in the stimulating company of the late Professor Meiklejohn, counting the plants on the Shiant Isles in early spring and finding 36 species in such an unpromising environment. On another occasion, when I came across one of the pea family I could not identify in an Uig cliff-face and have since been unable to find it again, I could have done with his sagacious advice. If I can arrange to visit Barra in spring-time, I never fail to catch my breath as I cross that shining, golden carpet of primroses at Eoligarry, surely unique in the Hebrides.

It is a sad fact of life that bird-watching and botanising, like angling, are really incompatable. How often does one, head down watching for, perhaps, the first long-leaved sundew or a rising fish miss the only rare bird of the day? Or head in air, watching a soaring eagle, step on the only bog pimpernel of the day?

Certain plants, like the Barra primroses are associated in the mind with certain places and in some instances are found only there. Some examples are the great reedmace of Bragar, the green hellebore and spotted catsear of the Stornoway woods, the delicate harebells of Cliff, the lesser butterfly orchid of Stoneybridge, the spring squill of Greian Head, the Scottish gentian of Melbost, the seaside pansy of Askernish. How much poorer we should be without them!

Pressed Plants as an Art by Hilda R. Robinson (G. Bell, Feb 1975)

Steller's Eider

George W. Steller must have been a man of many parts. A German naturalist of the 18th century, he discovered five unique and very different species, all called after him, a sea-cow, a sea-lion, a sea-eagle, a jay and a duck.

It is with the last I am concerned for it is the only one of Herr Steller's discoveries which, as far as I know, has visited our islands. In fact, only about seven Steller's eiders have been recorded in the United Kingdom. The latest of these has been a great attraction to all bird-watchers visiting South Uist since it first arrived in 1973.

In 1977 on a visit to that island, I spent my lunch hour at Peninerine looking for it again. I had had the good fortune to be shown it in July 1973 by the local warden of the National Nature Reserve at Druidebeg, without whose kind and expert assistance I should doubtless have missed it, for it was in moult and looking rather shabby.

Common eider abound on the sea off South Uist and, when not in moult, the drakes are quite unmistakable, being larger than the mallard and possessing an immaculate black and white plumage and a bold Grecian profile.

It was with a group of common eider that this stranger from Alaska or Siberia has spent the last three years and amongst them that I looked for him. Many times had I paid a visit to this very place in order to see him in his breeding plumage and always come away disappointed.

According to the book, he should be two-thirds the size of a common eider drake and more like a long-tailed duck than an eider, so he wouldn't be all that easy to pick out in the sea that was running.

There were many gulls about, together with shelduck and mallard; the beach was moving with countless waders, redshank, ringed plover, dunlin, sanderling, and purple sandpipers. Two grey seals floated, head above water, supremely indifferent to the breaking waves and pestilential gulls.

Suddenly, I saw the Steller's eider beside a drake common eider just before they sank into a trough. But I kept the glasses trained on the spot and obtained several glimpses of him between waves before it was time to go.

Petrels 1

The most common of the petrel family is a bird which most people probably pass off as a seagull. The more observant will notice, however, that its flight and appearance are quite different from a gull's. This is the fulmar petrel. A relation of the albatross, its wings are longer and narrower than a gull's which at once means that it is a soarer and glider rather than a flapper! When observed from a boat at sea, the fulmar's flight, following the contours of the waves, and its distinctive beak, grey back and white head and under-parts distinguish it clearly from all other birds.

It is strange to realise that 100 years ago, few people in the U K had seen a fulmar and yet the inhabitants of St Kilda depended upon some 25,000 pairs for oil for their lamps, feathers for export and for their main food supply. Suddenly, and for some reason upon which ornithologists are not yet agreed, fulmars began to colonise the rest of the U K from the north west.

One theory attributed the spread to an increase in the St Kildan stock due to plentiful supplies of whale and fish offal discarded by the western world's growing fleets of deep-sea whalers and trawlers. Another, to the rise in Iceland of a special type of fulmar able to exploit the different climatic and breeding conditions peculiar to the British Isles. Whatever the reason, there was reckoned to be about 25,000 pairs in the Western Isles and about 306,000 pairs in the British Isles in 1970 and there is now scarcely a part of the British coastline where one cannot watch these graceful birds.

Fulmar petrel

Petrels 2

They used to be called "Mother Carey's Chickens", but who she was, nobody seems to know for sure. Some say a sea witch on whom the storm petrels attended; some that "Mother Carey" is a corruption of Mater Cara (Dear Mother — or the Virgin Mary) under whose special protection the petrels were supposed to be. Anyway, this tiny creature, only 6½ inches long, weighing scarcely an ounce and the smallest web-footed bird, was seen by the ancients to be in need of providential help since it seemed never to come ashore to breed like other birds and was therefore assumed to do so on the ocean deep.

It came to light only in recent times, in fact, that in the breeding season these petrels, the storm and Leach's fork-tailed petrel, its slightly larger cousin, are nocturnal and fly into their nests after dark and depart before dawn. This, together with their preference for remote island sites such as St Kilda, Flannans, Sula Sgeir and North Rona, explains why they were never seen on land.

It is a memorable experience to listen to their character-istic recognition calls on say, North Rona, in the gathering dusk in June as they drop, bat-like, out of the sky to a nest in the rock crevice or wall, an echoing cry coming from the mate deep within, and pick up the peculiar musky smell exuded by all petrels. Robert Atkinson, in his book, *"Island Going",* gives an evocative account of similar experiences when visiting the offshore islands of the Hebrides in his boat "Heather" which many in Carloway and Stornoway will remember.

In autumn when the adults and young are making their way back to the Atlantic wastes for the winter, a westerly gale may cause the weaker birds to be cast ashore or to take shelter on board a handy ship. If they are not past hope, it is possible to revive them after a short rest in warmth with a course of fish oil from a tin of sardines for example fed by means of a syringe. When ready for release, since all petrels have difficulty in walking, the bird must be tossed upwards in a favourable wind near water when it will shake itself before circling to gain height and orientation and then disappear seawards.

Walk along any clifftop at almost any time of the year and sooner or later a fulmar will pass so close to you that you can see the individual feathers lifting in the updraught and surely agree with me that the fulmar has one of the most attractive expressions in the bird world.

But do not try to approach a nesting bird too closely or you will recieve a jet of foul-smelling oil directed with astonishing accuracy from an open bill. Gulping motions are the prelude to this very effective measure and a warning it is well to observe. This is the oil which the St Kildan used in his cruisgean.

Although the sea cliff is the natural nesting place of the fulmar, they sometimes use old buildings. Anyone entering the bothan on Sula Sgeir or the village houses on North Rona, for example, would be well advised to ensure that there is no fulmar within or he is in for a heart-stopping fright as the bird competes for the use of the narrow entrance in its hurry to get out.

I have had the good fortune to treat six stormy petrels successfully in this manner during the last twenty years.

Like the fulmar petrel, the storm and Leach's petrel feed on plankton and fish offal and the stormies often follow ships for this purpose pattering along the surface, when one can see why they are called petrels. Their webbed feet and wings enable them to "walk" on the water with more enduring success, however, than did the faith of their namesake, one Simon called Peter.